FORGOTTEN COAST

Coastal Traditions of Britain and Ireland

VOL 1 The Coast in The Past Series
ROBERT SIMPER

Published by Creekside Publishing

ISBN 0 9538506 2 5
Copyright Robert Simper 2002
Printed by Lavenham Press Ltd
Lavenham, Suffolk

By the same author

Over Snape Bridge (1967)
*Woodbridge & Beyond (*1972)
East Coast Sail (1972)
Scottish Sail (1974)
North East Sail (1975)
British Sail (1977)
Victorian & Edwardian Yachting from Old Photographs (1978)
Gaff Sail (1979)
Traditions of East Anglia (1980)
Suffolk Show (1981)
*Britain's Maritime Heritage (*1982)
*Sail on the Orwell (*1982)
Beach Boats of Britain (1984)
Sail: The Surviving Tradition (1984)
East Anglian Coast and Waterways (1985)
Suffolk Sandlings (1986)
The River Deben (1992)
The River Orwell and the River Stour (1993)
Rivers Alde, Ore and Blyth (1994)
Woodbridge: A Pictorial History (1995)
Essex Rivers and Creeks (1995)
Norfolk Rivers and Harbours (1996)
Thames Tideway (1997)
River Medway and The Swale (1998)
In Search of Sail (1998)
Family Fields (1999)
Rivers to the Fens (2000)
Voyage Around East Anglia (2001)

Robert Simper has written twenty-seven books as well as having a business career. He has also contributed to many other books, notably three chapters in *Chatham, Inshore Craft* and has written regularly for two nautical magazines. He was a founder member of the Old Gaffers Association and was later the President. He is chairman of the Dawn Sailing Barge Trust and on the committee that is building a replica of the Anglo-Saxon Sutton Hoo long ship. He has lived for forty-three years by a creek on the East Coast and has a cottage apartment in Cornwall and sails an 1896 dipping lugger.

Cover Coble *Gratitude* at Whitby
(Coble and Keelboat Society)

Contents

Chapters

Introduction

To see the first streaks of daylight at the beginning of a new millennium we drove down to Shingle Street, a hamlet on the Suffolk coast. It was still dark when we arrived and we crunched across the shingle to the water's edge where a slight sea was breaking lazily on the beach. Around us we could hear the excited voices from other parties who had also come to this easterly place to witness the beginning of a new millennium. In fact it seemed a bit of an anti-climax. There was a slight haze over Hollesley Bay, and no sign of the sun rising on a new era. Slowly the night was replaced by daylight. Someone in our party had brought champagne, so we drank that from paper cups and then retreated to the warmth of our homes.

This had been just the beginning of another, in this case rather mild, winter's day, but the world had moved on to another chapter in its long complicated history. Shingle Street is typical of the hundreds of villages and towns around the coast of the British Isles. Until World War II this hamlet had been the home of long shore fishermen and a few labourers who had made a precarious living from the bay in front of them. All that has been forgotten and the row of houses along the shingle ridge has become mainly holiday and retirement homes.

The traditional way of life dependent on the sea, which reached a peak in the late nineteenth century, vanished in many places in the twentieth century. A rise in living standards and advancing technology swept away the customs and dialects of the coastal people. The days when just about every village and town had its own special type of work-boat are almost gone, but in some places these strong local traditions have lingered on into the twenty-first century. In other areas there are societies and movements dedicated to keeping alive the traditional boats and customs of the past. Long may everyone hang on to their regional identity.

When my son Jonathan and I had the 1904 Suffolk beach boat *Pet* restored in 1981 we only found one man who remembered how to sail this type of dipping lugger. Anyone restoring a similar type of craft now is unlikely to find anyone with real knowledge of the old ways. They can of course relearn the old ways and many people have set out to rediscover the best from the past.

The aim of this book is to record some of the forgotten working practices of the age of sail and oar, and something of the places where the traditional way of life has managed to survive. It is not necessary to record a detailed picture of every place, for most seafaring communities already have at least one book devoted to their past. Instead, by describing some of the old working customs, a general picture can be built up of the whole coast. It seems worthwhile to make a record of the old ways before they slip over the horizon of time and become beyond recall.

Since 1972 I have written a series of books covering various rivers and sections of the coast of the British Isles and I have drawn on material collected over those decades. I have to thank a number of people for talking about the old days. Peter Herbert, as a young man in the 1950s, was master of the West Country auxiliary ketch *Agnes* and had a long career in coastal shipping. In 2001 he was still going to sea delivering ships. Also in the West Country, Alun Davies kindly took me out dredging for oysters under sail at Falmouth. Here, by keeping alive the art of dredging under sail, which is hard manual work, the oyster stocks have been successfully conserved. The art of sailing a dipping lugger has been revived in Cornwall, but at Beer, on the south coast of Devon, the old and the new revival eras did just overlap. Alan Abbot, whose father and grandfather had fished in luggers off the open beach, helped to revive dipping luggers for recreational sailing with an easier to handle rig.

There were Brixham trawlers working under sail until just before World War II, but when the 72ft (21.95m) sailing trawler *Vigilance* returned in 1997 there was no-one left who had sailed in one. The re-learning of these old skills has aroused great local interest so that the past has a purpose in giving people a real sense of identity with the area they live in.

On the East Coast there are many people used to handling Thames barges under sail. The working and revival ages overlapped here. The same is true of the Essex smacks. No-one revives the appalling living conditions of the old fishing villages, although most people regret that the old close-knit communities have melted away.

On the Humber there was again an overlap in working and the revival ages, all in one man, the Humber keel skipper Fred Schofield, who passed on his knowledge of sailing these most difficult craft. Up on the Coble Coast, as I called it in *Beach Boats of Britain,* I have had help from Amble coble builder Hector Handyside, and George Featherstone and Edgar Readman of the Coble & Keelboat Society. While on the fishing boat scene generally I have learnt from Mike Smylie and the 40+ Fishing Boat Association. At Deal Tom, Ben and Jack Burnham took us out in their boats. On the West Coast of Ireland, Dan Graham helped with Dingle Currachs and Dick Scott and Martin O'Brien showed us the Galway Hookers. On the editorial side my thanks go to Diana McMillan and my wife Pearl.

In many ways the modern world is becoming a better and safer place, but some of the old ways have a strong pull on the modern imagination. It could be that by blending the past and the present a strong sense of local identity can be kept alive. I certainly hope so.

RS
Ramsholt

Source of photographs. Michael Emmett 3. Colin Fox 7, 9. Carol Twinch 16. Scottish Fisheries Museum 45. Peter Stibbons 19. Jonathan Simper 20. Humber Keel & Sloop Preservation Society 23, 24. National Maritime Museum 55. Scarborough Marine Engineers 30. F.E. Sutcliffe 32, 33. E. Philip Dobson 35. Rev.H.S. Ross 39, J.R. Buchan 47. Dan McDonald 48, 49, 53, 54. Shetland Museum 50, 51. Robert Shortall 64, 67. Richard J. Scott 65, 68, 69. Dan Graham 71. National Trust 97. David Hawker 105. Sea Breezes 58, 70. Gwynedd Archives 79. R. J.H. Lloyd 77, 81, 83. F.E. Gibson 96. Alan Abbott 108. Old Gaffers Ass. 115. Peter Herbert 91, 92, 104. Colour photographs of the new trawler were supplied by MacDuff Shipyard Ltd. and the Eastbourne boat by Ron Keyte. The remaining photographs are from the authors collection and newer ones taken by him and Flamborough coble Paul L. Arro.

The Coble *Star of Bethlehem*, with a Northumberland 'dodger' over the bow, at North Sunderland, 1988.

The sailing barge *Nellie Parker* off Mersea Island beating up the River Blackwater.

Map of the British Isles

Chapter One

ESTUARIES IN A LOW COAST

The Thames Estuary to the Humber

1. 'George Murrell's lifeboat', about 1910. This craft was a Great Yarmouth salvage yawl, re-named the *Grace Darling* to attract the trippers. Getting afloat is very much a part of the way of life of an island race. Southend on Sea, at the mouth of the River Thames, was the nearest place most Londoners could get on the water. In the Victorian and Edwardian period there was a large fleet of tripper boats taking holidaymakers on trips during the summer.

2. Low tide in the creek at Old Leigh. On the right is the bawley *Virona,* a type of craft evolved for shrimping in the Thames Mouth, while further up the creek is a Thames spritsail barge discharging at a wharf. The flat bottomed barges were highly successful at trading into the shallow tidal ports around the Thames Estuary and up the East Coast to the Humber.

3. An Edwardian regatta day at Maldon on the River Blackwater with the town's oyster smacks about to get under way to start a race. In the Edwardian era there were no major industries at Maldon so that the local barges concentrated on farm trade taking straw, hay and mangolds to London for the street horses. Some barges continued in the mill and timber trade but the stackie barge trade died off in the 1920s.

4. Brightlingsea, at the mouth of the River Colne in 1934 with the sailing barge *Anglia* being hauled on to the hard. A fishing smack is lying out in the main channel while over on the St Oysth shore are two of the ketch smacks, known as the 'skillingers' after the island of Terschelling, which had been used for deep water oystering.

5. **Above:** By tradition the Mayor of Colchester, seen here on a sailing smack in 1973, hauls the first dredge of the season every autumn. This is because Colchester owns the riverbed and in the past the oyster fishery was a lucrative venture for the town.

In the nineteenth century all the Essex rivers had oyster fisheries, but the Colchester Oyster Fishery based at Brightlingsea was the best known. There were beds of cultivated oysters all the way up Brightlingsea Creek, but the Company headquarters were in Pyefleet behind Mersea Island.

5a. The Maldon smack *Fly* getting under way for a smack race in the Pyefleet, 1990. This Essex smacks were often built in yacht yards and were yacht-like, while bawleys were built on the barge yards and took on their characteristics.

7. The 77ft (23.47m) spritty barge *Orion* at Green's Brantham Mill on the River Stour. Although the *Orion* only loaded 100 tons she carried the full coaster's rig of a topsail and bowsprit jib because she was making a long passage up the Essex coast when bringing imported Manitoba wheat from the Royal Docks, London to Brantham.

Only a small barge could get up to Brantham and even then it called for tremendous physical effort. When the barge arrived at Mistley the skipper went home, leaving the mate to lower the mast and un-ship the bowsprit. The two Lucas hufflers then came aboard to 'poke' the barge up the tortuous two-mile channel to Brantham Mill. The barge could only get under Brantham road-bridge on the neap (low) tides and when she arrived at the mill, the mast had to be raised up again so that the hatches could be opened. To go back down river, often loaded with flour, the mast had to be lowered and then heaved up again in time for the skipper to make the next passage to the Thames. The *Orion* averaged 18 days on the round trip to the Thames.

The last freight to Brantham was delivered by *Orion* in 1938. Brantham Mill was burnt down in the 1960s and the site became an industrial estate. In 1971 the tidal Stour was dammed at Cattawade and it is now difficult to believe that sea-going craft ever went up there.

6. Left: The Harwich-built wooden spritsail barge *Marjorie* 'turning' (bargeman's term for tacking against the wind) deeply loaded in 1904. She was bound with imported grain from the London Docks up to the mills at Mistley on the Essex River Stour. Normally a barge this size was sailed by two men, sometimes with a boy acting as cook, but the *Marjorie* also has a party making a holiday trip aboard.

The Thames sailing barges were developed out of the flat bottomed, flat sided barges used in the eighteenth century to take cargo from the Pool of London inland past Oxford. These were cheaper to build than the older double-ended clinker barges and had flat sloping 'swim head' bows which tended to lift the hull so that they could operate in shallow water.

The early nineteenth century Port of London relied on barges moving cargo from the ships to the warehouses so that there was tremendous pressure to create a really efficient form of river transport. By adding the spritsail rig, with sails controlled by winches, to the flat bottomed barges with leeboards, the Thames Spritty barge was born.

8. Harold Robertson, skipper of the Mistley barge *Redoubtable*, in about 1930. The *Redoubtable* was a large spritty that loaded 180 tons to go to sea, with a crew of just two men, or 220 tons in the river. She was a very beamy barge, built to carry very bulky cargoes to the cattlefeed mills at Mistley, and had little sheer and a low bow to reduce the windage so that she could turn up narrow rivers and lonely creeks. Skipper Robertson had a reputation for making fast passages in *Redoubtable* and once blew out eleven topsails in twelve months. The owners did not mind too much because it proved he was 'having a go', trying to deliver more freight and not sitting around 'wind bound'.

The deeply-loaded steel sailing barge *Repertor* just below Pin Mill in the River Orwell, about 1950. The
ny appearance of the sails shows that they have been 'dressed' with the traditional preservative mixture of
d oil, red and yellow ochre and as a fixer, urine. The Kent barges had dark brown sails.
This helped to prolong the life of the sail, but it never dried and came off on the crew's clothing.

11. Seven spritsail barges in the Ferry Dock, Woodbridge about 1907. The barges on the left had brought in barley which was discharged by the 'humpers' who carried sacks on their backs down a plank to a horse and cart. The carts then went up the road to the Maltings in Quay Street. Woodbridge is one of the hundreds of small 'lost ports' around the coast of the British Isles, that no longer have any commercial traffic. Woodbridge had blossomed as a port in the Tudor period when it became a shipbuilding centre, but the difficulties of getting ships over the bar at the entrance to River Deben killed the port. The last freight to Woodbridge was coal to Sun Wharf in the steamer *Maloo* in the hard winter of 1940. She was held up at Waldringfield for some time because of the ice in the river. The Ferry Dock has been used by yachts and houseboats since but became so badly silted up that work began on scraping it out in 2001.

10. Left: Ipswich Dock in about 1935. On the left is the Cranfield Bros. sailing barge *Excelsior* which would have discharged imported wheat at their mill at the head of the dock and then sailed back to London for another freight. In the centre is R. & W. Paul's Home Warehouse. Paul's sailing barges brought important barley in sacks from London in the summer. These were emptied into the Home Warehouse so that the whole building was filled with loose grain. In the winter this barley was moved to the maltings and made into malt. Most sailing barge crews were paid with a share of the freight money but as the Ipswich owners almost used their barges as warehouses, their crews were paid on a weekly basis. After World War II the firms that were 'seeking' freights steadily sold off their 'sailormen', but as speed was not important for the Ipswich mill barges the port retained the last fleet of merchant sailing vessels. Paul's sold their last sailormen, *Marjorie* and *Anglia,* in 1960. After this Cranfield's *Venture* and *May* carried a few freights under sail until being sold and the *Spinaway C* undertook lightering and was finally sold in 1967. The Pin Mill-owned *Cambria* actually carried the last full freight under sail when she delivered animal feed to Ipswich in 1970. In 2001 Peter Dodds Faversham *Mirosa* and Andy Harman's St. Osyth's *Edme* both sailed without engines.

12. The RNLI Aldeburgh lifeboat *City of Winchester*, being launched off Aldeburgh beach. To operate this pulling and sailing lifeboat called for the strength and co-operation of most of the longshore fishermen of the town. The crew in the lifeboat were hauling her out through the breakers on a hauling-off line, while other men, ashore, were pushing the lifeboat off with poles. When the lifeboat returned the fishermen then manned the hand capstan at the top of the beach and dragged her back up to her station.

14. Suffolk longshore fishermen at Dunwich in 1983. The number of boats working off open beaches reached a peak in about 1890 when there were over 355 places around the coast of the United Kingdom that were beach landings of some description. The number of working beach boats steadily fell as the inshore stocks of fish were depleted.

Dunwich is one of the few places where the number of boats has stayed about the same from the Victorian period, but erosion has completely altered the coast. Over the centuries the entire medieval walled town of Dunwich and its natural harbour have gone into the sea.

13. Left: The Aldeburgh long shore fishing boat *Dorothy May* returning from long lining for cod in 1981. Working off the open beach, the Aldeburgh boats are limited, particularly in the winter, to the number of days they can put to sea. To add to their difficulties there is an inner shoal or bar just offshore running right up the Suffolk coast and this has to be crossed before reaching the open beach.

In 2000 seven boats were working off Aldeburgh beach, but as they only landed small qualities of cod and flat fish they were only economic because they could retail direct to the public from their huts. In the past the longshore herring, which come inshore during the cold weather, were the main fishery of Aldeburgh. Until World War II the Aldeburgh Fishermen's Guild operated a large smoke house in Oakley Square and then for a few years after the war the Guild sent away a railway truckload of fresh herring every day.

Before the railways opened up wider markets, smuggling had been the main occupation of most coastal villages. In 1776 Lord Orford said 'every man in Aldeburgh, but the parson, was a smuggler'. Just up the coast the saying is 'Pakefield had one poor parson and they buried him alive': from the time when the Pakefield parson was taking a walk on the beach when a smuggling craft was 'making a run'. The smugglers buried the parson up to his neck in the beach so that he could not go and warn the customs officers. At Alderton, to the south around Orfordness, the parson had probably been involved in the smuggling because goods were landed near Shingle Street, taken up Beach Lane and hidden in the church. This smuggling stopped when the customs built a watchtower on a house in Alderton Street to keep an eye on the beach.

15. The fishermen's 'beach village' at the bottom of the cliff at Southwold. The beach boats were hauled up the beach by hand capstans, known here as 'bulls'. This beach village has been completely eroded away and the fishing boats moved around to the mouth of the River Blyth. All that remains of this community is the Sailor's Reading Room, built on the cliff top in 1864. The idea behind the Reading Room was that the long-shore fishermen would have an alternative place, to the public houses, to spend their evenings.

17. A group outside G. & A. Gunn, the Lowestoft fish merchants, about 1926. It was said that every fisherman at sea provided jobs for five people ashore. At this time Lowestoft, and the rival East Anglian fishing port of Great Yarmouth, are reputed to have had hundreds of smokehouses. Many were small back yard operations smoking herring.

16. Left: The trawling smack LT 1273 leaving the Trawl Basin at Lowestoft under sail in about 1925. The skipper is standing at the long tiller while the crew are heaving on the peak halliard to set the mizzen. As they are still in the harbour, the bowsprit has not yet been run out. On the Lowestoft trawling smacks all the ropes could be led to the steam capstan as this was used to do all the heavy sail handling.

At sea the trawl was down for the six hours of a tide and then it was hauled up by the steam capstan. The skipper sailed the smack by taking the halliards and sheets to the capstan to trim the sails, while the mate and crew handled the net and sorted the catch. The crew only helped the skipper with really heavy tasks such as reefing. While in port a watchman was paid to keep the capstan fire alight so that it could be ready for the really heavy job of hoisting the mainsail and running out the bowsprit. The trawling smacks stayed at sea in all weathers, riding out gales hove-to under heavily-reefed sails.

There were two different fishing communities in Lowestoft. The trawlers that worked in the North Sea all the year round, mainly trawling for plaice, were manned by men living in the town, while the drifters only worked in the autumn herring season, and were mainly manned by men from the longshore fishing villages and the farms.

18. The Great Yarmouth dandy *Our Boys* in about 1900. At both Yarmouth and Lowestoft such herring drifters were still called 'luggers' although they had been given a gaff ketch rig. In the early nineteenth century three-masted Yarmouth luggers were often called 'salt carts' because they preserved their catch by salting them at sea. Once landed, the salted herring was then hung up in the smokehouses and smoked over a smouldering fire of oak sawdust to make them more palatable. Dandies like the *Our Boys* went to sea at dusk, laid out about a mile of drift nets and then returned in the morning so that their catch could be taken fresh to the big cities by the railways.

18a. 1702 Yarmouth herring lugger.

19. High tide on Cromer beach in about 1902. The crab boats are just going off, but at low tide they had to be carried down to the water by putting oars through 'orrucks' (oar ports). The men are filling up bags of shingle for ballast and this was tipped over the side as the boat was loaded with the catch. The North Norfolk fishermen wore dark blue 'ganseys', knitted by their womenfolk, having one for work and another for 'Sunday best'. They also wore leather boots, which were very warm, but they had to be oiled regularly to try and keep them watertight. All East Anglian beach boats are launched bow first and after coming ashore are turned round clockwise 'with the sun'. The men who manned the sailing crabbers cursed any of the young men who did not follow this custom, because they believed that going into the sun, flying in the face of the devil, would bring bad luck.

Local versions of the double-ended clinker hulls were used around the coast of the British Isles from Anglo-Saxon times until the eighteenth century. After this an enormous variety of local boat types began to evolve. However, North Norfolk men kept the beamy clinker double-ended hull because it was ideal for riding through the steep breaking seas on their long shallow beaches. Stratton Long of Blakeney produced the first fibre-glass Norfolk crabber in 1973, a copy of the 16ft (4.9m) *Star of Hope* built by Emery of Sheringham in 1906. The following year Richard Davies advised Stratton Long which 22ft (6.70m) Cromer boat to take a mould from, which led to the *Paternoster* being built. In 2000 there were thirteen traditional wooden and fibre-glass crab boats working off the beach, but in 1997 John Davies had broken with over a thousand years of tradition and bought a fast catamaran for crabbing.

20. In 1981 there were only three North Norfolk crab boats working full time from the West End landing at Sheringham and another two at the End East. Here on a wild winter's afternoon, a crowd of cheerful fishermen were hauling boats up, on a block and tackle, clear of the waves breaking high up the beach. The tackle was made fast to an iron ring and five men ran up the road hauling while four put slides under the boat to steady its progress to safety.

21. A beam trawl being hauled aboard William Stringer's Boston smack *Fred & Norah* in 1927. The trawl is being hauled aboard using a backstay. Sailing smacks had halliards and running rigging hooked into iron rings in the deck so that they could be moved and used for hauling from a different angle. Due to the strong currents in The Wash, between ever-shifting sandbanks, very few fish came in to feed. Because of this the fishing boats operating from King's Lynn and Boston concentrated on trawling for shrimp and loading shellfish on the banks.

1. The author and his grandson Harry at Old Leigh with the *Reminder,* last of the wooden Leigh boats, and the modern steel cockler *Renow'n.* The creek at Leigh-on-Sea is only a harbour at low tide, at high tide the sandbanks at the mouth of the Thames are covered and a considerable sea can break on this exposed foreshore. However, in 2001 Old Leigh was the home of nine steel cocklers, that went out twice a week, and a number of trawlers.

2. The Leigh cockler *Renown 1V* rounding Southend Pier on her way back from suction dredging cockles on the Maplin Sands. The Leigh cocklers are a type of local workboat still evolving. In the Victorian period cockling started with men going down to the sandbanks to collect cockles by hand in 'galleys', old warship boats bought from the Royal Navy Dockyard at Sheerness. These were replaced by sailing cocklers, with centreboards, such the 34ft (10.36m) *Mary Amelia* in 1914, which had to be fast to get down and back in one tide. These were followed by motor-sailers, still with centreboards, such as the 35ft (10.67m) *Endeavour* in 1924. By the time the wooden 43ft (13.29m) *Theodore* was built in 1946 she was a motor craft but still had sails. Hand-raking of cockles was replaced in 1967 by suction dredgers and this resulted in larger, steel craft being built.

3. Spritty barges lying off Gravesend for the 2001 Thames Sailing Barge Match. This race was first held in 1863 and claims, after the America's Cup, to be the world's second oldest sailing event.

4. The Thames spritty barges *Repertor, Reminder* and *Phoenician* sailing with the 'in-board' staysail rig in the 2001 Pin Mill Sailing Barge Match. The flat-bottomed barges with spritsail rig controlled by winches are highly versatile. They are able to make long sea passages and sail up narrow creeks.

5. The steel spritty barge *Xylonite* racing. In the rivers and docks the barges had their bowsprits lifted, which allowed them to manoeuvre in a smaller area. The Thames spritties were very effective craft with the waterline length of around 80-90ft (24-27m). Smaller barges didn't develop so much speed and on larger barges the leeboards became difficult to handle.

6. The *Waverley,* the last sea-going paddle steamer, going alongside Clacton Pier in 2001. The pier at Clacton, like many other piers, has a berth for excursion steamers to pick up passengers.

7. The Great Yarmouth shrimper *Horace & Hannah* sailing off Lowestoft in 1998 with the Hastings boat *Argonaut* astern. The Yarmouth shrimpers were day fishing boats and they returned to port in the afternoons in time for the shrimps to be boiled and sold for the trippers' teas.

22. Everard's mulie barge *Britisher* discharging grain at Gleadell's Mill, Morton Corner on the River Trent in 1905. The whole cargo was being worked by hand with men carrying the sacks ashore on their backs across planks.

22a. Humber sloops racing in the Barton Sloop Regatta.

24. The wooden Humber sloop *John & Annie* discharging coal at Franks brickyard at South Ferriby. In the nineteenth century the amount of manpower needed on coastal craft was cut down by introducing winches. This sloop has a halliard winch on the side of the hatch coamings and the man and boy are working a winch forward to lift out the baskets of coal.

The Humber sloops were mostly owned in small havens along the Lincolnshire shore of the Humber and adopted the gaff sloop rig because it was more effective on the open estuary. The last Humber Sloop Regatta was sailed in 1929. Most of the Humber keels and sloops were motorized in the 1930s and they had their sails taken off at the start of World War II.

23. Left: The skipper and his wife helping the Humber keel *Danum* through a shallow 'shy rack'. The Humber keels, with two square sails, were extremely effective craft for working the narrow rivers and waterways connected to the River Humber. When passing through locks, the foot of the square sail was just lifted up and when they had reached the new water level the sail was dropped down again. Out in the Humber, the keels could only sail with the very strong tide. The swirling brown tide was sometimes so strong that if a keel touched a sandbank it ran the risk of rolling right over.

The Humber estuary cuts into the side of England with numerous small rivers flowing into it. This was a natural system for water-borne transport and goods were imported and exported through the docks at Hull. From Hull, the keels, which were known by the size of the canal locks, took goods to the industrial towns far inland in Yorkshire. The clinker double-ended billyboys, the sea-going version of the keels, took cargoes to North Norfolk and the Thames Estuary.

25. Fred Schofield aboard the wooden Humber keel *Annie Maud* at York in 1976. Fred had once skipper-owned Humber keels and he had just rigged out the *Amy Howson* again for the Humber Keel and Sloop Preservation Society. In this way the knowledge of how to handle these complex craft was passed on to another generation.

25a. The wooden Humber sloop *Mafeking* ready for launching at Brown & Clapston, Barton-on-Humber in 1900. After Brown retired in 1912 the yard was run by four generations of the Clapston family and they built their last wooden sloop, *Peggy B*, in 1935.

Chapter Two

THE COBLE COAST

Spurn Head to the Tweed.

26. The harbour cobles at Bridlington, loaded with trippers, in about 1908. As there was little wind, the cobles are being punted out with long poles. There are fifteen cobles in sight and they carried up to thirty-six people each. In the Edwardian period, the railways transported thousands of 'holidaymakers' to resorts all around the British coast. A 'trip around the bay' was the high point of any seaside holiday.

From Spurn Head up to Berwick, a type of open clinker craft, known as a coble, was used for fishing, piloting and taking 'holidaymakers' on pleasure trips. In Yorkshire, coble is pronounced cobble, while further north in Northumberland the pronunciation is 'coobel', which was the local medieval word for an open boat.

The cobles have a very deep forefoot to grip the water, while they are flat-bottomed aft. When beaching, the high bow was kept facing the seas while the flat-bottomed stern allowed them to go in stern first and wash right up on to the beach.

27. Bill Pickering at the tiller of the Bridlington coble *Three Brothers* leaving the harbour in 1988. The oper cobles' deep forefoot and shallow stern can make them difficult to sail. Certainly sometimes when they were rowed, two men pulled on the 'rowing thoft' (thwait) while a third man pulled on an oar over the stern to keep the coble going straight. The long rudder acted as a centreboard when sailing, and in a strong breeze one man was ready to let the halliard go and drop the sail if a gust threatened to capsize the coble.

29. Richard Emmerson's *Imperialist and Prosperity,* with the Flamborough varnished hull and orange colour inside, hauled up at the North Landing, in 1982. The other two cobles here were R.W. Emmerson's *Summer Rose* and the *Spring Flower.* The first engine was installed in a Flamborough coble in 1920 and the last sailing coble finished in 1939. The last coble builder in Flamborough was Hargreaves 'Arg' Hopwood, who died in 1939. He was something of a legend because he produced beautiful cobles single-handed, but worked behind closed doors and would not show anyone else the art of building by eye.

Richard Emmerson, a third generation to work a coble from Flamborough, said in 2000 that there had been good cod fishing grounds about two miles off Flamborough Head in the 1980s. Each coble worked four long-lines, each baited with whelks on 400 hooks, and this traditional method did not endanger the fish source. It seems that since then the huge powerful trawlers, with their sophisticated fish-finders, have almost emptied the North Sea of cod.

28. Left: Crab pots being unloaded from a small Yorkshire coble at the North Landing, Flamborough in about 1920. The catch was taken from the Landing up the steep path to the village on the backs of donkeys. In 1794 twenty fishermen were drowned coming ashore at the North Landing and most winters cobles, or sometimes men, were lost. In an on-shore gale this Landing becomes a boiling mass of white water. Because of the difficulties of hauling the cobles up the very steep beach a steam capstan was installed in about 1900. A Crossley, horizontal single cylinder petrol-paraffin engine, replaced this in 1912 and then this was replaced by a diesel engine. At the South Landing, horses were used to recover the cobles. Some families kept a coble at each landing and used them according to the weather. In the Victorian period Flamborough was a remote place with its own dialect and customs. In the autumn the village held the 'Raising of the Herring' when the women dressed up as men and walked through the village singing. The fisherfolk were very superstitious and kept what was probably an old pagan custom alive, even though most people attended church or chapel.

30. The new 27ft (8.23m) double-ender *Isis* SH 278 was built, larch planks on oak frames, by Scarborough Marine Engineers in 1998 for fisherman Richard Buchanan to fish off Filey beach. The *Isis* was intended to be used for commercial fishing in the winter and for angling trips in the summer. Filey has a long shallow beach and the double-ender's pointed stern is essential as it parts the short seas that roll in behind a boat when it lands.

31. A small Scarborough mule with reefed sail returning to her berth in about 1910. She was sailing with a dipping lugsail abacked. It would have been dangerous to have the sail pressing on the mast in a strong wind but she has her oars shipped ready to help her round in the harbour. The double-ended fishing boat was a separate type of craft that worked on the north-east coast alongside the coble.

Wooden sailing ships were built and owned in Scarborough and there was also a large fleet of craft engaged in the herring fishery. The Scarborough yawls, drifters similar to the Lowestoft luggers, developed out of the three-masted 'five man' luggers. These used to discharge their catch into cobles to be landed on the beach, but because the smell and activity upset the summer visitors they were obliged to use the harbour.

32. Penzance and St Ives luggers with cobles being rowed in the background at Whitby in about 1890. Although the luggers in the herring fishery moved around the coast following the shoals, they all fiercely retained their local identity so that, although fished in the same waters, the Cornish boats would have been totally different to those of Whitby.

South of Redcar, the north Yorkshire coast is a line of cliffs and the only port is Whitby where the tiny Esk estuary just manages to form a natural harbour at the bottom of its valley. In the eighteenth century Whitby was a port of considerable importance and between 1753 and 1837 whaling ships sailed from here to Arctic waters. It is still a major fishing station and in 1999 sixteen trawlers between 54ft (16.46m) and 74ft (22.56m) were owned and operating from the harbour. There were about twenty smaller boats, with an average length of 33ft (10.06m), which operated static-gear. That is trammel and gill nets moored on the seabed for the fish to swim into, and pots for crab and lobster. In 1975 there were thirty wooden cobles fishing from Whitby, but in 2001 there were only four cobles.

33. Young women at Whitby in about 1895 'skaning mussels' so that they can be used as bait on the long lines, carried by the fishermen, for cod. The longshore fishermen in the nineteenth century depended on their wives and family to do the work ashore.

Even when motor trawlers came in, the Whitby men followed the old custom of throwing money into the sea, to pay Neptune, at the start of each trip. The medieval church suppressed belief in the Norse sea gods, but sailors remained very superstitious, because when undertaking anything as unpredictable as making a voyage under sail, they needed 'good luck'.

35. Right: Cobles at Staithes in about 1960. In 1817 the Rev. George Young wrote that there were seventy cobles at Staithes working from the seaward end of the tiny tidal inlet at the mouth of the Colburn beck. There were also fourteen larger decked 'five man' boats. In 1861 there were 120 cobles at Staithes and later the railway ran three special trains a week to take fish away. The cobles at Staithes came ashore stern first, and were then pulled clear of the water using the oars as skids, on Seaton Garth beach. Men, women and children did the pulling as there were no horses available.

Although a breakwater was built to protect the landing, Staithes declined because steam trawlers and drifters from the deep water harbours gradually took over their fishing grounds. The last decked boat, *Charity,* gave up in 1920, and the big 35ft (10.67m) cobles went soon afterwards. In 1923, the *Mizpah* was the first Staithes coble to be fitted with an engine. Because of erosion cobles were no longer able to be kept in front of Seaton Garth and the remaining boats, mostly double-enders, had been kept in the Colburn.

34. Tony Goodall, building a coble at Sandsend in 1982. The boatyard was the old station yard in which Tony's father had been stationmaster. No plans or moulds were used in the construction of a coble. In the 1970s there were six yards where Whitby cobles were built and Tony Goodall was the last one building them. From 1953-91, when he built the *Incentive* WY373, Tony Goodall, who retired in 1995, had built about thirty cobles ranging from 28ft (8.53m) to 37ft (11.28m) in length.

The motor harbour cobles of Whitby tended to be larger and to have more beam than the Northumberland beach cobles. Because a coble is flat bottomed aft, the early motor cobles had problems with damaging their props when beaching. In the 1930s the Whitby coble-builder William Clarkson solved this problem by housing the prop in a 'raised ram tunnel'. Housing the prop in a tunnel not only stopped it from being damaged, but increased the efficiency. Whitby fishermen were also the first to have their cobles decked forward and in 1960 the Whitby Shipbuilding and Engineering Co. built the 37ft (11.28m) *Jane Elizabeth* which was the first one to have a wheel-house.

36. The cobles at Cullercoats in 1982, including the long narrow Northumberland coble *James Denyer* in the centre and the Whitby *Argonaut,* with a foredeck and wheel-house, on the left at the back.

In 1818 there were ten cobles working from the sheltered cove at Cullercoats and this rose to forty-three winter cobles in 1878. Cullercoats went on to have the largest fleet of beach cobles on the north-east coast because the men got work in the shipyards and went fishing when there was a shortage of work.

In 1982 there were five cobles working full time from Cullercoats. These cobles went about one and a half miles offshore 'until the piers opened' (that is the piers on either side of the Tyne mouth), then they were on the 'soil', an area of clay seabed. They also went after salmon in the summer and long-lining for cod in the winter.

38. The 36ft (10.97m) *Joanne D* of Blyth, nearing completion at Harrison & Sons yard, Amble in 1980. The Amble yard of James & John Harrison was started in 1870 and originally built square-rigged sailing ships for the coal trade. They switched to cobles in about 1912 and by 1976 had built 396.

On the left, standing near another new coble, is master coble builder Hector Handysides. He started at Harrison's in 1948 and first worked on building the coble *Eileen & David* for Newton by the Sea, where there were then seven cobles. After this he worked on cobles continually, sometimes building three at a time. No plans were used. The construction of the coble started with the 'ram' (keel), and after this, every measurement was determined by this first plank. The builders carried the formula for the coble's construction in their heads. Hector Handysides built his last fishing coble, the 34ft (10.36m) *Three Sisters R,* for drift-netting for salmon from Newbiggin, in 1986. The building of new wooden traditional boats continued around the coast until the Government stopped giving grants for new craft. After this the few remaining fishermen had to find a cheaper form of craft.

When Tony Goodall launched the *Incentive* in 1991 it was thought this would be the last wooden coble, but in 2002 Steve Cook at Whitby built the 23ft (7.0m) *Bay Jo.* This coble was built for Leonard Oliver to fish from Robin's Hood's Bay, a beach landing in cliffs south of Whitby.

37. Left: The coble *Silver Jubilee,* one of twenty-two boats working off Redcar beach in 1982. The cobles are lined up on the beach retailing fresh fish. Sales could only be made on the beach and they were not allowed to retail fish beside the road. Later, tractors towed the cobles away on their trailers and called in at the filling station to replenish the coble's diesel on the way.

Before World War I the pilots of the River Tees, just to the north, were Redcar men who used to go off in fast double-ended boats. The sandy beach at Redcar is very shallow and double-enders were always popular because they were better at coming through waves breaking astern.

39. Fishermen pulling a salmon net aboard a sea coble at Spittal in about 1925. From the River Tweed north-wards, up the East Coast of Scotland a flat-bottomed coble of about 22ft (6.70m) was used for netting salmon along the beaches. These clinker rowing boats had a soft up-turned bow to meet the sea. Salmon fishing took place between February 15 and September 14. Sections of the Tweed are divided up into salmon fisheries and the rights to the salmon fishing date back to the medieval period.

39a. Cobles hauled out at Craster about 1900 before the harbour was built. The cobles were so important to the survival of Craster that in an on shore gale everyone, including pregnant women, and children, had to turn out and haul them up the road to safety.

Chapter Three

THE FISHERMEN'S HARBOURS

The Scottish East Coast, Highlands and Islands.

40. The fifie *Reliance* with her decks piled high with cotton drift nets. Her proud crew are wearing leather boots and the typical clothing of fishermen from the east coast of Scotland around 1900. The straight-sterned fifies hailed from around the Firth of Forth while the zulus, with sloping sterns, came from the ports further north around the Moray Firth. These boats followed the herring shoals from the Hebrides down to Great Yarmouth.

In 1975 the Scottish Fisheries Museum, Anstruther bought the 70ft (21m) fifie *Reaper* and returned her to a two-masted lugger, maintained and sailed by the Museum's Boat Club. The *Reaper* was built in 1902 by Forbes, Sandhaven for drift net fishing and great lining (long lining). While most of her type were broken up she survived, because after World War II she was sold to Zetland County Council and used as a power vessel, to move general cargo around the Shetland Isles.

41. A father and son unloading lobster creels from a lug yawl at Crail, Fife in 1913. Fishermen used the lug rig because it left the centre of the boat free to work the gear and the mast could be lowered at sea when drifting or rowing. In the eighteenth century most small craft had the spritsail rig, but the lug was adopted where drift net fishing was common. A dipping lug was simple to work where there was plenty of sea room.

The rocky sea bottom made Crail a crab, lobster and sea urchin centre. The tiny harbour at Crail, which dries out at low tide, is dangerous to enter in bad weather. In the background on the right is the crane used in bad weather to lower boards down across the 21ft (6.4m) entrance. The fishermen lived in stone two-storey houses in the streets behind the harbour. These had an outside staircase or 'forestair' while the ground floor was used as a net and gear store.

42. Fishermen and their families beside a rowing and sailing boat at Auchmithie in 1904. On the East Coast of Scotland when the men were going off fishing for the night their womenfolk 'kilted their coats' (tucked their dresses and petticoats up) and waded barefoot into the surf with the men on their backs. The practical reason for this was that the men wore leather boots, that were not watertight, and had they gone to sea with wet feet they would not have been able to stand the cold during the night. In the morning the womenfolk came down to the beach and carried the men ashore as they had no effective way of drying the men's boots.

8. Richard Matthew's grp *Northern Star.* This North Norfolk crab boat was at Weybourne Hope in 2001. The sea is deep off Weybourne, but most of the North Norfolk beach landings are very shallow which create incredibly short dangerous seas. Until World War II the larger Norfolk boats were taken down to the water with horses, but tractors replaced them.

9. The Norfolk whelker *Knot* in Blakeney Harbour, 2000. In the Victorian period smacks from King's Lynn were used for whelking off the north Norfolk coast, but the boats from Wells-Next-the-Sea took over the fishery. The Wells fishermen purchased old Cromer crab boats and ex-naval launches for whelking, but later the local builders started to produce larger clinker motor craft. The largest of these double-ended whelkers was the 30ft (9.14m) *William Edward* in 1949 and in 2000 a mould was taken off her to make the first grp whelker.

10. The Humber Keel and Sloop Preservation Society's steel keel *Comrade* at Hull. A keel built in 1923 by Warren, at New Holland. The Society also has the 61ft (18.59m) gaff-rigged sloop, *Amy Howson,* built by Joseph Scarr at Beverley in 1914.

11. The coble *Three Brothers* leaving Bridlington with coble *Kate & Violet* ahead.

12. The 28ft (8.53m) coble *Madeleine Isabella* off the North Landing, Flamborough in 2000. This coble was built by George Cambridge at Hartlepool in 1912 for William Handyside of Beadnell, with larch planks on elm frames. She was the last sailing coble built for a Beadnell fisherman and arrived by train. The final part of the journey was on a farmer's flat hay bogie. Later William Handyside moved to Amble where his grandson Hector became master coble builder at Harrison's.

In 1985 Hector bought his grandfather's coble which was then being used for fishing from Paddy's Hole, Teesmouth. Over the next fifteen years he rebuilt her, but due to poor health he was unable to sail her and she was sold to Steve Emmerson of Flamborough.

Another sailing coble that Hector Handyside rebuilt was the 30ft (9.14m) sailing coble *Sweet Promise,* built by George Cambridge in 1906. Ninety year old Percy Douglas gave Hector the coble providing he totally rebuilt her. In 1978 she was relaunched with a dipping lug rig and 6cwt of ballast down the centreline and 80lbs of moveable ballast just for trimming when sailing.

13. The 70ft (21.3m) wooden trawler *Concorde* built by the Watt's Macduff Shipyard, Macduff in 2000. The Watt family originally built fishing boats in Aberdeen, but in 1945 they moved to Gardenstown and Banff. The harbour dries out here so they were restricted to building fishing boats no longer than 65ft (19.81m). In 1965 they purchased the Macduff shipyard where it was possible to launch larger vessels. In 1980 Macduff Shipyard Ltd. employed seventy people but by 2000 this number had risen to 120 and they were regularly building wooden or steel vessels up to 92ft (28.04m) long. This family-owned yard has become the most successful fishing boat repair and building yard in the British Isles.

43. A wooden fishing vessel under construction at Makay's, Arbroath in 1973. On the East Coast of Scotland wooden fishing vessels were built long after other fishing areas had gone over to steel hulls. The wooden boats can last a long time, the 43ft (13.10m) fifie *Isabella Fortune* AH 153 spent her first eighty-five years fishing from Arboath. Built as a lugger in 1890, when she changed ownership in 1908 for £65, following Scottish custom, the seller had to give a new fore lugsail as a 'good luck piece'. She was first fitted with an engine in 1919 and in about 1980 Hobson Rankin restored the *Isabella* and used her as a cruising yacht until 1997 when she was bought by the Wick Society and rebuilt from the waterline upwards.

43a. Salmon cobles at the deserted fisher village of Boddin Point, south of Montrose, in 1988. In much of Britain, when fishing declined, tourism and non-local residents created new communities, but in Scotland many coastal settlements were simply abandoned.

45. Montrose fishermen, rowing a salmon coble. Montrose is at the mouth of the South Esk River and had a fishing community across the narrow entrance at Ferryden. Fishing had died out at both Montrose and Ferryden by the inter-war years when fishing became concentrated on the deep water ports with fish markets. The commercial salmon fisheries were very heavily controlled and regulations clealy stated that only salmon cobles could be used to work the seine nets. These flat bottom salmon cobles, basically clinker punts which were once used as far south as the Tyne, appear to have come from the same origin as the cobles of the Northumberland coast. By 2002 the fly fishing interests had closed almost all the commerical salmon coble fisheries, although there were some still operating in Caithness.

44. Left: The ruined harbour at Auchmithie in 1988. On the hilltop above the harbour is the lookout shelter where the women waited and watched for the luggers to return from fishing.

In the late eighteenth century there were about fifteen boats fishing from the beach at Auchmithie. This number steadily increased so that by 1880 there were forty boats employing seventy fishermen, but after this the number declined. Because of the poverty in Auchmithie, farmer's wife Annie Gilruth campaigned to get the small harbour built, about 1896, but there was never enough income to pay for its maintenance. When the harbour started to wash away the fishermen gave up and moved to Arbroath, which has a very good harbour. They took with them the practice of smoking salted haddock to make 'smokies'. Originally this was done at Auchmithie where 'smoke pits' were created by sinking barrels into the ground with a sack over the top to control the smoke. At Arbroath, 'smokies' are briefly smoked over a hardwood fire in back yards.

46. The Lowestoft steam drifter *George Baker* entering Aberdeen in about 1935. The herring shoals arrived in Scottish waters during the summer and the fleet of herring drifters gradually moved south to Scarborough and Whitby and in the autumn down to the East Anglian fisheries of Great Yarmouth and Lowestoft. The 'fisher lassies', women who gutted and salted the herring and packed them in barrels, and the herring smokers, followed the fleet as it moved down the coast.

47. Right: Launching the wooden 65ft (19.81m) *Constellation* FR294 from J. & G. Forbes at Sandhaven in 1964. Skipper Joe Buchan found that cruiser-stern boats lacked deck space and while he was on a minesweeper, he decided that the square stern would create more space. The idea for a forward wheelhouse came from one he had seen on a boat at Shields and the ideas were combined to produce the *Constellation*. In 1974 Joe Buchan had a larger 74ft (22.56m) *Constellation II* built, again incorporating more new ideas. Although the Scottish skippers are very progressive, many have kept loyally to wooden hulls.

9. Inshore fishing yawls at Findochty in 1938. The scaffie yawls *Vine, Lively, Boy Joe* and *Jessie* were all still being used for fishing under sail. Findochty is one of many stone harbours on the Scottish East Coast which was built in the late eighteenth and early nineteenth century at the start of the great fishing era, but as inshore stocks of fish were exhausted fishermen gave up.

8. Left: The three-ton fishing yawl *Willing Boy* BCK 251, with a well-cut lugsail, entering Portknockie in August 1938. They have the oars ready to pull her up into the berth. At this time a few of the older men were still working sailing yawls.

The land-owning Lairds built many of the villages and harbours on the East Coast to develop the rents from fishing. Portknockie fishing village was started in 1677 and the harbour built in 1692. By Victorian times it was one of the major herring-fishing centres on the Moray Firth. After World War I the harbour had to be enlarged to take all the fifty-eight steam drifters owned here, but after World War II fishing faded out.

50. Herring nets aboard the Shetland herring boat *Queen Adelaide.* The big steam capstan, that was used to haul the nets in, can be seen behind the men. The drifters from Lerwick had zulu hulls developed from the Moray Firth boats, but because they had to beat against the wind up Bressay Sound to reach Lerwick they had gaff mainsails. In around 1900 the number of boats engaged in the herring fishery was breathtaking. There were sometimes as many as 800 boats fishing out of Lerwick.

The largest of the Lerwick herring boats was the 60ft (18.29m) *Swan,* built by Hay & Co. in 1900. The *Swan* fished under sail until 1935 and finished in the 1980s as a motor fishing vessel at Hartlepool. She was then taken back to Lerwick, totally rebuilt, and began running trips under sail.

52. The Ness yole *Ivy*, abandoned near the Pool of Virkie on Mainland Shetland in 1982. The Ness yoles were used to fish in strong tidal waters off Sumburgh Head. The yole had a dipping square sail and when rowed the men sat as near as possible amidships to keep the weight out of the fine ends of the boat. Like the Shetland model, which has long been raced at Lerwick, there has been a revival of interest in the Ness yole and the *Ivy* is one of the boats that have been restored.

In 2002 Lerwick was the largest herring and mackerel landing port in Britain. The small Shetland Island of Walsey, population 1,100, had a highly successful fleet of super trawlers, loading up to 1,600 tonnes, operating in the mid-ocean.

51. **Left:** The far haaf (ocean) fishing station at Fethaland in the Shetland Isles in 1895. There were about fifty of these stations around Shetland and fishing from here in open boats in the Atlantic was always a very dangerous form of fishing. The worst disaster in the haaf fishery was in 1832 when no less than thirty-two sixerns were lost in a single NNW gale. Again in 1881 a sudden and terrible gale in July caught the haaf fishermen at sea on the far ground. In one night fifty-eight men and boys were lost, leaving thirty-four widows and eighty-five children.

The sixerns, six-oared open boats of about 30ft (9.14m), were used in the haaf fishery. They had square sails which were swung around the mast when they went on a fresh tack. Since there are no trees in Shetland, these boats were originally shipped in kit form from Norway. When boat-building started in Shetland their boats were based on the Norwegian craft. Because of the high winds the 'Shetland Models' are often kept in 'noosts', shaped pits on the foreshore, to prevent them from being blown away and damaged.

53. Here, under the shelter of the jetty, a net is being sorted out on the line fishing skiff *Dawn,* at Kilchattan, Bute in 1923. In the nineteenth century many of the beach landings in the Highlands and Islands of the West Coast of Scotland had small stone piers built to give the boats some protection. In the background is the Loch Fyne skiff *Deer II.* The first Loch Fyne skiffs were built in 1882 for herring fishing and over the next thirty years some 540 were built around the Clyde.

54. Above Right: The Arran smack *Betsey Crawford,* owned by the Crawfords of Corrie, discharging coal on the open beach at Blackwaterfoot on the Isle of Arran in 1934. The steam puffers took all the trade through the Crinan Canal to the Western Isles, but until World War II the sailing smacks, mostly fitted with small engines after 1931, were able to compete with them from the Clyde ports to the islands of Arran, Bute and Milford and the open beaches on Kintyre. About twenty were owned on Arran and another eight on Bute. Some of these were ex-fishing craft, with finer lines which were much faster under sail, but could not discharge on the beaches.

The last Arran smacks built were the *Betsey Crawford* and *Fairy Dell* in 1897. The *Fairy Dell* was skipper-owned by Captain Angus Kerr of Lochranza, Arran. Once, the mate came on deck in a gale to find the skipper had gone overboard and after this it was believed that Kerr's ghost would come to the aid of the smack in times of danger.

55. Right: The Arran smack *Hunter,* discharging coal at Kildonan, at the southern end of Arran, in 1908. The Arran smack's hulls were deep with full sections and were immensely strong, which enabled them to take the ground fully loaded. The smacks were about 45ft (13.71m) long and loaded about 35-40 tons. The middle section of the rail could be lifted out to make it easier to discharge and they towed a 'punt' astern. The punt was a heavy open dinghy able to hold about three-quarters of a ton of coal. Sometimes these loaded punts were sculled ashore for the coal to be shovelled into a cart while the horse stood up to its belly in water.

56. The tiny pointed-stern tops'l schooner *Petrel* discharging coal on the open beach at Carsethorn in the Solway Firth. The *Petrel,* built at Liverpool in 1852, only loaded 38 tons and was reputed to be the smallest British trading schooner. Owned by Captain Willy Robson of Carsethorn, she made countless trips across the Solway Firth with potatoes and returned with coal, before being broken up in 1932.

57. The little harbour at Ballintoy, County Antrim with Rathlin Island on the horizon. On the Causeway Coast the Portrush fishermen work from a double-ended boat for salmon fishing which is lowered over the cliff. During the summer, between March and September, Atlantic salmon, looking for a river to swim up and spawn in, swim from east to west along the north coast of Ulster. In the 1960s 350 tonnes of salmon were landed each year, but by 2000, because the fish were being caught out in the Atlantic, this had fallen to about 10 tonnes.

Chapter Four

WESTERN WATERS

The Irish Sea and the Atlantic Coast

58. The wooden motor ketch *Emily Barratt,* just after crossing the Appledore Bar in about 1953. The *Emily Barratt* was the last vessel built at Millom, a small iron ore port on the Duddon estuary. The first vessel built here was the schooner *Nellie Bywater* by William Thomas in 1873. He had moved to Millom from Amlwich, a schooner-building centre in Anglesey.

Launched in 1913, the *Emily Barratt* was the last British merchant schooner built, but was soon altered to a ketch so that she could have a smaller crew. In 1928 *Emily Barratt* was bought by George Welsh of Braunton, one of the four places inside the Appledore bar which continued, like Arklow, to concentrate on operating small coastal sailing vessels, not as pure sailing vessels, but fitted with low-powered auxiliaries. The *Emily Barratt* finished trading in 1959, after which she had a long-chequered career that ended when she was taken to Barrow-in-Furness in 1987. Regrettably, instead of the original plan to save her, she was later broken up.

59. The Morecambe Bay prawner *Nora,* being rowed back to Overton in 1894. These fast, handy, day fishing craft originated for shrimping in Morecambe Bay, but were later used from the Solway Firth right down to Cardigan Bay. In Liverpool they were called nobbies, probably from nobby meaning cheap timber.

The Crossfield family built most of the nobbies. This family started at Arnside, Westmorland in 1853 and gradually settled all along the West Coast. The last nobby they built is reputed to have been the 28ft (8.53m) *Comrade* in 1936, and in 1989 John Neary was still fishing her, under sail and motor, from Liverpool.

0. A Morecambe Bay nobby racing in the Fleetwood Channel in about 1922. When they were shrimping or rawling, these craft had a crew of two, but carried a larger crew for races. They were such fast sailing craft hat businessmen used to charter them for racing.

1. These schooners at Port St Mary's, Isle of Man have their canvas sails out to dry, because if they were towed wet they would have developed mildew and become rotten. The coastal sailing vessels had to try and match their passages from port to port in good weather. In bad weather they sought shelter. Port St Mary was a good place to shelter while on passage in the Irish Sea.

62. Manx nobbies, the local herring luggers, and trading schooners at Castletown, on the Isle of Man in about 1905. Castletown was the Manx capital until 1874. Castle Rushen dominates the harbour and stands on the site of a Viking stronghold. In 1840 there were 600 Peel registered boats employing 3,813 men in the herring fishery. The practice aboard the Peel nickeys, two-masted luggers developed from visiting Cornish drifters, was to sail in the early afternoon. Peel Harbour was sheltered by the hill and castle and there was often little wind. To get out of the inner harbour a rope from each boat was run through a pulley, placed on the end of the quay. The boat was then hauled at speed and shot out into the outer harbour.

Once at sea, the skipper gave a signal and all the crew took off their hats and offered a silent prayer. As the fleet moved south in sight of the Calf of Man, a bottle of rum was handed around and each man had a horn measure-full. The skippers watched out for the tell-tale sign of birds feeding on the water to show where the herring shoals were. Once the nets were shot the men dropped on their knees to offer another prayer. At dawn the nets were hauled and if a boat had too many herrings to take aboard a horn was blown to attract another boat to come and off load on to them.

Every boat had an arrangement with a pub so that throughout the season the fishermen and their wives could go there any time for a drink. The bill was settled at the end of the season from the income from the season's catch. There was no fishing on Saturday or Sunday.

63. Above Right: The 104ft three-masted motor schooner *Windermere* off Maiden's Quay near Waterford on the River Barrow about 1950. She was one of the last sailing vessels involved in the coal trade from the River Mersey across to southern Ireland. The *Windermere* was built in 1890, like the *Kathleen & May,* at Connah's Quay.

The *Windermere* was sold to owners in Arklow, County Wicklow and traded alongside the motor schooners *J.T. & S., Invermore* and *De Wadden.* The 92ft (28.04m) *Invermore* and *J.T. & S.,* which were built at Arklow in 1921 with engines and cruiser sterns, were the last three-masted schooners constructed for the Home Trade.

64. Right: The 116ft (35.36m) three-masted schooner *De Wadden,* in the dry dock at Merseyside Maritime Museum, Liverpool in 1989. This steel schooner was built at Waterhuizen, The Netherlands in 1917, and was bought by Halls of Arklow five years later. After World War I many small British and Dutch sailing vessels were sold to Irish owners. The *De Wadden* was the last of the Irish motor schooners trading. In 1961 she was sold to an owner on the Clyde for sand dredging. She was running sand from the Kyles of Bute to Dunoon until 1977 and was then used for angling trips until 1981 when she was bought by Merseyside Maritime Museum for long-term preservation.

65. The schooner *Windermere*, laid-up at Arklow in 1956, after she had hit the Tusker Rock near Porthcawl and was withdrawn from trade. Wheelhouses and the winch houses were added to British, Irish and Baltic schooners when they were fitted with engines.

66. The *Brooklands* sank near the Tuskar Rock in 1953. She was built in 1859 by Kelly at Dartmouth for E.Vittery as the tops'l schooner *Susan Vittery* and traded with fresh fruit from the West Indies. When steamers took over the fruit trade she, like many deep-water schooners, fell back into the coastal trade. The schooner was rigged out as a three-master. This made smaller sails that required less labour to handle. The schooner had been sold to Crean of Cork in 1923.

SCHOONER LOST OFF EIRE COAST

From Our Own Correspondent
DUBLIN, Tuesday.

The 94-year-old schooner Susan Vittery, last of the old Irish sailing vessels, sank three miles north of Tuskar Rock lighthouse, off the south-east coast of Co. Wexford, late last night. She sprang a leak near the Saltee Islands on Sunday.

The crew of four spent eight hours in an open boat in St. George's Channel. They were first blown towards the Welsh coast and then back to the Tuskar Rock. They were rescued by lifeboat.

Picture—P10

THE SUSAN VITTERY, the 94-year-old Irish schooner which foundered on Monday night near Tuskar Rock lighthouse, off the south-east coast of Ireland.

57. The three-masted 99ft (30.18m) tops'l schooner *Brooklands* of Cork, discharging at New Ross in about 1940. The cargo gaff was aloft on the foremast and the cargo, probably coal, was being shovelled into baskets, hauled up to deck level by hand winch and then tipped into a lighter alongside. The *Brooklands* carried cargoes under sail only until 1946. She was the last pure sail schooner or ketch 'in either islands', as the schoonermen called Ireland and Britain.

58. Galway hookers loaded with peat at the City Docks, Galway about 1960. The larger hookers only loaded 12-15 tons of turf, but they were very capable craft carrying peat, general cargoes and passengers on the Atlantic Coast. The hookers from the Connemara coast took turf to Galway and returned with groceries and other goods.

Because the road system in Connemara was very poor the Galway hookers were the last sailing cargo craft in Northern Europe. In the 1920s there had been about 400 hookers, but lorries gradually replaced them. Their last trade was taking turf for household fires out to the three Aran Islands. In 1974 John Jimmy McDonagh's 38ft (11.58m) Connemara hooker *An Mhaighdean Mhara (The Mermaid)* carried the last turf freights from Callahaige pier out to Aran.

69. The 38ft (11.58m) Galway hooker *An Tonai* racing in Casla Bay in 1975. The turf trade to Aran had only just finished when the revival era started with a series of races around Galway Bay. This led on to the 39ft (11.89m) *MacDare* being built at Kinvara by Bill Crampton in 1981 and she was the first new hooker built for over fifty years. Since then the number of hookers has increased and they have become frequent visitors to maritime events in Western Europe.

There were four different types of hookers which were known in the Irish language as the Bad Mor pronounced Bawd Moor (big boats), Leath Bhad pronounced La Wawd (half boats) and the smaller fishing craft Gleoiteog, pronounced Glowchug, and the lug-rigged Pucan pronounced pookaun.

71. Curraghs, ready to race at the Dingle Town Regatta Day in 1960. Dingle Regatta, sponsored by Guinness, became the centre of curragh races. At Dingle, and at the annual parish curragh races, local honour was at stake and the days ended with good crack and drinking.

The curraghs were still being built for everyday working use when the racing championships were started at Salt Hill in 1954. The curraghs used for regattas are sleeker than those used for fishing off open beaches and are known as 'racers'.

After the devastating nineteenth century famines the people in western Ireland turned much more to the sea as a source of food. The traditional lore on the Dingle Peninsula was that the 26ft (7.92m) canvas skin curraghs, known here as 'naomhogs' or canoes, were introduced from South Clare about 1830. In 1921 there were about four hundred West Kerry curraghs, but the mackerel fishery ended and the number dropped to eighty in 1934. In 2002 there were around forty curraghs on Dingle, and although Eddie Hutchinson was building new ones, there were mostly old ones at Ballydavid and Brandon Creek. The most active curraghs appeared to be at Dunquin, on the most western point of the Europe, where six were kept for potting at the foot of the steep path down the cliff. All were fitted to carry outboards. In 1953 the last fourteen people on Great Blasket were moved to the mainland and each family was given a house and an acre of land in Dunquin. Up to two hundred people had once lived on the six Blasket islands and rowing a curragh across the strong tides some three miles to Dunquin or over twelve miles to Dingle had been their only link with the outside world.

70. Left: A curragh beaching on Inisheer, one of the Aran Isles off the coast of County Clare, 1956. The curragh's hull has a light wooden frame with a canvas outer skin. They survived on the West Coast of Ireland because they were inexpensive to build and operate and on a coast with few natural harbours they were light enough to be lifted in and out of the water. The Aran curraghs had high bows to meet the large seas and long shallow sterns so that their buoyant hulls came right up to the water's edge and the men stepped ashore with dry feet. The rowers sat low in the hulls to give them stability in the large Atlantic seas.

On the Irish-speaking Aran Isles the curraghs were used for fishing and getting the steamer passengers ashore. Although slightly different, the curraghs on the coast between Donegal and Kerry were widely used for fishing and general run-abouts. The larger 24ft (7.31m) Aran and Kerry curraghs carried a small lug sail, but they were mostly rowed with bladeless oars on a single throle or 'dowl' in Irish.

Chapter Five

CARDIGAN BAY AND THE SEVERN SEA

West Wales to Hartland Point.

72. The 82ft(25.15m) topsail schooner *Sarah Evans* ashore on the north Cornish coast at Portreath in 1932. She had anchored for shelter but was blown on to the beach. All the crew were saved, but the following day the schooner was just a mass of firewood on the water's edge.

In the late 1920s Helen Bruce had gone on holiday and at Fowey she saw 'the little schooners which had gone to Newfoundland' lying for sale. She bought the *Sarah Evans,* which had been built in 1877 at Porthmadog for taking salted dried cod, stock fish, from Newfoundland to the Latin countries. Under Captain Ben Harris of Bideford, the *Sarah Evans* was kept sailing in the coastal trade, but at a loss. Captain Harris suggested that a vessel with an engine be purchased. Mrs Bruce then bought the *Mayals,* an iron three-masted schooner with a low-powered engine. In 1931 the *Mayals* was anchored in Milford Haven 'windbound' waiting for a favourable 'slant' of wind, when she was run down and sunk by a steam trawler. At the inquiry it was shown that the trawler's skipper was so drunk that he had to be carried on to the bridge. So ended Helen Bruce's contribution to keeping sailing ships going.

73. The launching of the three-masted tops'l schooner *Gestiana* at Porthmadog in 1913, the last of the Western Ocean Yachts for the Newfoundland trade. So called because they were very smartly kept up and traded across the Western Ocean (Atlantic). Other ports on the Clyde and in the West Country specialized in Western Ocean Yachts in the Newfoundland trade, taking dried cod to the Latin countries. From the end of the 1870s new schooners for the Newfoundland and slate trades were regularly being built at Porthmadog.

The 95ft (28.96m) *Gestiana* was built by David Williams of Madoc Street, for shareholders in Porthmadog and when she was lost on her maiden voyage, while on passage from Newfoundland to Cape Breton Islands, this was a major financial setback to Porthmadog's schooner fleet. The fleet, with its Welsh-speaking crews, completely vanished in the decade after World War I, leaving the quays and slate sheds empty.

74. The crew of the 95ft (28.96m) schooner *John Pritchard,* a three-masted tops'l schooner built at Porthmadog in 1904 for the Newfoundland trade. In 1916, during World War I, the *John Pritchard* was sunk in the Mediterranean by an Austrian submarine. This was at the end of an era when small, remote ports all around the coast had been building, owning and manning small sailing ships for the ocean trades.

75. The tops'l schooner *Ellen Beatrice,* built at Aberystwyth in 1865, alongside the pier at Aberdovey. The summer visitors were using the pier for promenading. The railways brought in visitors, which changed the character of a place, but ended social isolation and created local revenue.

The tops'l schooner was a piece of nineteenth century technology. The lower fore and aft sails allowed the vessel to point fairly close to the wind and only required a small crew to handle them. While the square sails on the foremast had tremendous pulling power, especially for down wind sailing, when tacking against the wind they could be 'abacked' (filled the wrong way) to force the vessel's head around on the new tack.

76. A cow about to be swum across the estuary of the Mawddach in 1885. Around the coast, cattle were swum across rivers and over to islands. A rope was put around the horns of the leading animal and once in the water the other cattle would follow her as she was towed across. Sometimes there were pounds beside the water in which the cattle were gathered in readiness for the swim.

14. The Galway hooker *Morning Star,* in Brittany in 1996. The turf carrying hookers had a smaller sail area because men had been killed by low booms. When coming into a pier the two men had to get the sails down quickly.

15. Struthan, Casla Bay, Galway about 1970 when Mike O'Brian was trading his hooker *An Tonai*, loading 6-10 tons of turf, from here across to Aran in the summer. The ten-mile passage out to Aran sometimes took just over an hour or all day if they had a row. There were two bunks under the foredeck and the cooking was done over a turf fire in a cement bowl.

The O'Briens of Shruthan started sailing passengers, often twenty-five people, across to Aran in *An Tonai*. This lead to Paddy O'Brien starting Island Ferries which owned five ferries in 2001 and at the height of the summer carried 3000 passengers a day between Rossaveel, Casla Bay and Aran. The *An Tonai*, skippered by Martin O'Brien, has been a frequent winner in the hooker races.

16. The 19ft 9ins (6.2m) *Yankee Jack* sailing at the Bristol Festival of the Sea, 1996. The spritsail rigge flatties were the workboats of the Somerset coast, but they had almost died out when builder Harold Kimb of Highbridge built the *Yankee Jack*. Her appearance at Bristol triggered off a whole new interest in this ty of local craft and resulted in more being built and a museum opening at Watchet.

17. Rebuilding the schooner *Kathleen & May* at Bideford West-the-Water on the River Torridge in 1999. T *Kathleen & May* was bought by the Maritime Trust and restored in the early 1970s, but it was said that sl was such an important craft that she should never risk going to sea again. Because she was not going to se and getting salt water on the timber, nor being maintained properly she was in serious need of a major rebuil Steven Clarke took her to Bideford, raised the funds to rebuild her and she made a voyage to Youghal, whe she once traded with coal, in 2001.

77. The *City of Birmingham* was one of the Aberystwyth pleasure boats that ran trips off the beach. Taking visitors on trips around the bay in the summer often brought in more cash than the winter fishing.

Inshore fishing from North Welsh and Cardigan Bay ports never developed on the same scale as in Cornwall or the Isle of Man, but most villages with a beach had some double-enders working in the herring season and nobbies worked from the estuaries.

78. Nobbies at low tide in 1935 at Aberaeron in Dyfed. Aberaeron harbour at the mouth of the River Aeron was created in the early nineteenth century by the local landowner, the Reverend Alban Gwynne. In the nineteenth century there was real poverty in many of the small ports and villages around the coast and some estate owners started projects to try and improve employment. The mountains cut off much of West and North Wales from the markets inland and made it very difficult to develop local economies.

79. Fishwives at Llangwyn, Pembrokeshire in about 1895. In many inshore fishing communities the women walked around the district retailing the catch. The fishwives of Llangwyn walked north to Haverfordwest with oysters and herring or twelve miles south to the market at Tenby on Carmarthen Bay. The fisherfolk of Llangwyn were considered a 'strange people', a race apart from the country people in the villages around them.

80. Tenby, on the south Pembrokeshire coast, in 1884. The sailing trawlers were from Brixham and they landed their catches in Tenby harbour from April to September. There had been a few trawling smacks owned in Milford Haven, but the locally-owned fleet did not really develop until the Great Western Railway opened the fish dock at Milford Haven in 1888.

31. As Tenby had strong connections with the West Country, many local boats were built 'over the other side'. Here in 1936 are the Tenby fishing boats *Myhew, Mary, Pretty Polly* and *Two Brothers*.

Tenby was a successful fishing port, thanks to the arrival of shoals of herring in Carmarthen Bay, from the fourteenth century, but the large steam vessels from Milford Haven gradually exhausted the local fisheries.

32. The Tenby lugger *La Mascotte* sailing past Caldy Island about 1935. At the end of the nineteenth century about forty luggers fished from Tenby, but by the 1930s only four were left under sail. These took visitors on trips during the summer and in the winter fished for bass 'behind the island' (Caldy).

85. Top: Pilot skiffs, as the Bristol pilot cutters were known, lying at Pill, in about 1910. On the right is the Harbour Master's office, with a flagpole, and Rowles yard, where many of the cutters were built, is just beside it. Pill was the home of pilots taking ships to Bristol.

83. Above Left: The oyster skiffs (smacks) off Mumbles, manoeuvring in 1922 at the start of their annual race. The foreshore is covered with ballast left from French ships that once came here to load iron ore from a small mine.

In the eighteenth century small open boats worked the oysters off Mumbles and then the fishermen bought smacks from Devon and Essex and by the late nineteenth century they were being built in South Wales. These smacks worked oysters in the winter and went trawling from Swansea and Carmarthen Bays in the summer.

The skiffs at Mumbles were kept in a small natural harbour, but the railway company got permission to fill this harbour in to make a seaside garden for summer visitors. The agreement was that the railway company would build a new harbour for the smacks, which they did, but there was no provision for them to maintain the harbour wall. When this washed away there was no shelter for the skiffs.

84. Bottom Left: The Barry skiff *Kindly Light* hove-to ready to put her pilot, in the punt, aboard a small steamer. It was the world's appetite for steam coal that caused the evolution of the Bristol Channel pilot cutters. Every sizeable ship needed a pilot to enter and leave the coal port. The pilots all operated independently, cruising in the Bristol Channel 'seeking' incoming ships. Once the pilot had boarded a ship the 'man' sailed the cutter home. Inward-bound ships knew which cutters to make for because of the sail marks. Swansea S, Neath N, Port Talbot PT, Barry By, Cardiff Cf, Newport N, Gloucester and Sharpness GS.

86. The trading ketch *Irene* in the River Tyne, in 1984. When she was launched in 1907 at Bridgwater she was the last trading ketch built in the British Isles. From the huge fleet of schooners and ketches in the Home Trade before World War I only a very few have survived and of these the *Irene* has been kept in sailing order by decades of hard work by Leslie Morrish.

87. Left: The Bristol Channel pilot skiffs *EMC* and *Pet* at Pill in 1937. When at sea these skiffs carried their punts on the port deck and had open decks which were good for working on. In the 1920s most pilot cutters were sold to become yachts, or broken up, so that by 1999 when races were resumed in the Bristol Channel there were only seventeen cutters left.

87a. The Bristol Channel pilot cutters *Olga* and *Mascotte* waiting for repairs at Tommi Neilsen's yard G l o u c e s t e r Dock, 1996.

90. The 98ft (29.87m) *Kathleen & May* was a pole-masted motor schooner laid up at Appledore in 1968. She was built in 1900, like the *Windmere,* by Ferguson & Baird at Connah's Quay, as a three-masted topsail schooner. Tom Jewel was skipper-owner of *Kathleen & May* until she finished trading in 1960. She was taken to Southampton to become a yacht, but Captain Davies brought her back to the River Torridge with the intention of returning her to trade, but she was just laid up on the mud. At the time the schooner was fitted with a valve by a film company which intended to sink her.

88. Above Left: The Landing on Lundy Island in 1984. On the right, hay is being brought ashore from the National Trust's ex-Greenland coaster *Polar Bear,* while on the left passengers are returning to the paddle steamer *Waverley.* Lundy was one of the last of the old-style beach ports until the jetty was built in 1999.

89. Left: The *Hilda,* a 116ft (35.36m) wooden barquentine, being towed out from the River Tyne just before she was cast off to sail into the North Sea. There were steam tugs at all larger ports to tow the schooners and small square-riggers in and out.

The *Hilda* was built by Pickard at Appledore in 1879 and became part of a fleet of vessels operated by C.W. Couch of St Austell. Her normal trade had been to take china clay north and return with coal. In 1930, when bound from the River Blyth to Cornwall with coal, she was hit and cut in two. She sank in two minutes but her crew just had time to jump on to the Hartlepool steam trawler *Kudos* that had sunk her. Dimly lit, slow moving sailing vessels were very vulnerable in the steamship age.

Chapter Six

ROUND THE LAND

The Cornish Coast

91. The auxiliary ketch *Agnes* leaving Bude, 1937. This little bluff-bowed ketch was officially built at Bude in 1904, but she was actually a far older vessel. In fact she was the *Lady Acland,* built in 1835, which was hauled ashore in Henry Stapleton's yard, cut in two and lengthened by 13ft (3.96m) and given a new keel. The Bude ketch *Wild Pigeon* was wrecked just outside the port so her main mast went into the new *Agnes* and her new mizzen was a spar from the Austrian barque *Capricorno* which was also wrecked on the north Cornish coast. With a crew of three, the Agnes traded to ports as far away as the Channel Isles, but while Bude-owned she mostly traded, summer and winter, down the coast between Hartland Point and Padstow, one of the toughest parts of the coast in the British Isles.

In 1919 the *Agnes* was sold to owners in Braunton, Devon and became part of the fleet of little motor sailers operating from the ports inside Appledore Bar. Because she was small, the *Agnes* traded from the Bristol Channel ports to coves and open beaches. She took coal freights to Watermouth, a cove east of Ilfracombe, and in about 1930 was almost wrecked. While waiting off St David's for good weather to enter Solva, the anchor cable parted and she went ashore on the rocks and her keel was scoured away to her garboards. Because she was very strongly built, her oak 3.5 inch (9cm) planks, which were tree nail-fastened (round wooden pegs), survived and she got back to Appledore for repairs.

92. The auxiliary ketch *Agnes* at Barry in 1955. She was loading 107 tons of wheat for Swansea. During World War II and for the years just after it there was tremendous demand for any ship to carry cargoes and the *Agnes*, although very small, kept working profitably with a 60b.h.p Widdop oil engine and a cut-down sailplan.

In 1955 the *Agnes* was skipper-owned by Peter Herbert and was carrying about forty dry cargoes a year, mostly grain from Avonmouth, Swansea amd Barry and 'down the land' to Padstow and Weybridge. She also took some freights across to Lundy Island. In 1957 the *Agnes* was sold for an 'adventure voyage' and was eventually lost on Barbados.

95. The Cornish gig *Newquay* leaving Newquay harbour for a race in 1954. The 28ft 11ins (8.57m) Newquay was built by William Peters at St Mawes in 1812.

In Cornwall the six-oar gigs were used for passenger-carrying, salvaging and taking pilots. They were also used for smuggling trips across to France because they could be rowed up into the wind if a Custom's cutter appeared. Similar gigs were built all around the coast of Britain for the same type of work, but the Peters family of Polvarth near St Mawes are credited with developing the Cornish gigs. Because the gigs were stored ashore in boathouses, between jobs, many have lasted an incredibly long time. The Peters' 31ft (9.45m) *Dove* of 1820, 30ft (9.14m) *Bonnet* and the 28ft (8.53m) *Slippen,* both of 1830 and several other Victorian gigs still survive.

93. Above Left: Clovelly 'long boom' smack anchored off the village with several of the other Clovelly smacks inside the eighteenth century harbour. The Clovelly trading smack *Ebenezer* used to carry 28 tons of coal from Newport and discharged at Bideford, Boscastle and Hartland and on the open beaches at Bucksh.

94. Left: The trading ketch *Ceres* entering Bude in heavy weather. When the *Ceres* was lost outside Appledore bar in 1936 she was 125 years old and had traded to Bude for eighty-four years.

The entrance channel to Bude, which dries out at low tide, is a dangerous haven to enter in a westerly or northerly wind. At other times, even in calm weather, a ground swell rolling in from the Atlantic closes the haven. In spite of the dangerous entrance, Bude harbour remained the main route in for bulk commodities for this part of northern Cornwall, until the railway arrived in 1898. At that time there were over twenty schooners and ketches owned in Bude, but as they were lost, usually trying to enter the haven in the winter, most owners didn't replace them. A further step in the decline of the port was when Stapleton's yard, which had built ten vessels between 1835 and 1878, closed in 1917. Only N. H. Trevaskis continued and he spent a great deal on keeping the *Ceres* going for the local coal trade. By the 1930s she was fitted with an engine and did not trade in the worst of the winter weather. After her loss the steel motor ketch *Traly* was purchased and she brought the last freight in to Bude in 1946. In 1967 the Council tried to close the lock into the canal but local opposition kept it open and in 2000 there were six inshore fishing boats working out of the Bude Haven.

8. Falmouth workboats dredging for oysters under sail on the East Bank, Carrick Roads in 1984. The Truro Oyster and Mussel Fishery, which controls the Carrick Roads and Truro River, is unique because its rules ban power boats from dredging oysters. This rule was introduced in the Victorian period to prevent steam dredgers from being used, but by using the inefficient sail boats or haul-tow punts it limits the number of oysters that can be taken in the limited hours of a working day. While many oyster fisheries were worked out once power craft were introduced, the 'no power' rule has proved a very effective conservation measure.

96. Above Left: The Cornish gigs *Serica* and *Dove* racing in St Mary's Sound, Scilly in 1968. Gig racing was revived in Scilly in 1962 and the *Serica*, built in 1967 on the lines of the *Bonnet,* was the first of a new generation of Cornish pilot gigs used for racing.

The working gigs raced each other to be the first to reach a ship and put a pilot aboard. Gig racing took place at regattas and was put on an organized footing when the Newquay Rowing Club was formed in 1921. However racing had almost died out by World War II, but at Newquay there was enough interest to keep the gig racing going.

97. Left: The Mount's Bay Barge at St Michael's Mount in 1994 just after she was rebuilt. This two-masted lugger was built of elm, with low sides for rowing, on the Lizard Peninsula in about 1790 to ferry Lord St Leven to the mainland at high tide. In 1840 she was used to ferry Queen Victoria ashore when she visited the island. In about 1900 a new barge was built and the old one was left in her boathouse until she was rebuilt.

Some of the wooden pleasure boats, that have been stored ashore in houses, have lasted an incredibly long time. The 25ft (7.6m) schooner *Peggy,* built in 1791 by the Quayles at Castletown, Isle of Man was used as a workboat, yacht and for ferrying people to the mainland. She was kept in a dock under the Quayles' house, forgotten until the 1930s. She is now in the Manx Nautical Museum in Castletown. Another craft stored in a boathouse free of fresh water was the 23ft (7m) Norfolk Broads lateener yacht *Maria,* built in 1827 at Great Yarmouth, and now in store in a museum there. The 16ft (4.8m) *Green Boat* was built some time at the end of the eighteenth century. She was used at the summer residence of the Wynn family at Fort Belan on the Menai Straits right up to 1986, when she became part of the collection of the Merseyside Maritime Museum.

99. Ron 'Hammer' Laity's fibreglass 28ft (8.53m) *Helen May* had only been dredging oysters in Carrick Road for a few days when seen here in 1974. In the Victorian period there are thought to have been up to fifty boats dredging in the winter season, but the fishery has always fluctuated with oyster stocks and market demands. In the twentieth century the highest number was forty five boats in 1922 and thirty five in 1969. The fisher averages around twenty boats, but after the oyster disease Bonamia hit the fishery in 1981 the number dredging fell to just five boats.

The Victorian dredging boats were a mixed bunch, but many were old sea fishing luggers converted to the gaff rig to make them handier. Like the luggers, the Falmouth workboats have straight stems and transom sterns, but have a shallow draft so that they can dredge on the 'banks' at low tide.

After World War II the oystermen assumed that their archaic fishery would die out, but in 1962 a hard winter wiped out most of the East Coast oysters and the prices rose. This gave oystermen the confidence to order new boats, first in wood, but to get them cheaper Terry Heard at the Tregatreath yard, Mylor Creek, started building fibreglass hulls. The first of the 28ft (8.53m) two-man workboat class began with *Melorus* in 1972 and the one-man 23ft (7.01m) started with the *Carrie* in 1978.

18. David Wakeley totally rebuilding Malcolm McKeand's 52ft (15.85m) Bristol Channel pilot cutter *Kindly Light* at Gweek on the River Helford in 1999. The *Kindly Light* was built in 1911 for pilot work and was converted to the yacht *Theodora* and then back to a pilot cutter.

19. Alun Davies hauling an oyster dredge, ready to sort out the catch on to trays on his 25ft (97.62m) grp Falmouth workboat *Iris Elizabeth*. Astern, *Boy Willie* is also 'drifting' down the East Bank, Carrick Roads, in 1999. The *Iris Elizabeth* has a 30hp engine that is used 'to get home' when mackerel fishing at sea.

20. The Falmouth workboat *Kindly Light* sailing 'back up' in Carrick Roads to begin another 'drift' back dredging with the tide, in 1999. That winter there were fourteen 'sail boats' working in the Truro River Oyster Fishery.

21. The 19ft 6in (6.01m) Gorran Haven boat *Albion* was one of five crab boats built in 1921. Gordon Couch rebuilt her at Gorran Haven in 1999. The crab boats of Gorran retained the eighteenth century spritsail rig, while in the nineteenth century most Cornish fishing boats went over to the dipping lug.

100. The start of the November 5 Silver Oyster Race for Falmouth workboats in Carrick Roads in 1984. In 1901 the dredgermen of the Truro River won a major legal victory giving them the right to use the foreshore. Because this ruling became known on November 5 the dredgermen have, since then, always taken this day as a holiday and raced their workboats. Because of the interest in the summer workboat races people started fitting them out primarily for competitive racing. This led to the creation of a separate class of workboats, the racers, in about 1974. They used spinnakers, hand winches and usually a far larger sail area than the dredgermen needed or could afford.

101. A Mevagissey-built lugger off the Cornish coast in about 1905. Mackerel drivers, the Cornish term for a drifter, could have their masts lowered when they were 'laying to their nets' at night. This reduced the rolling and made life very much more comfortable for their crews.

From the sixteenth century Cornwall's main fishery was the pilchard. All along Cornwall's three hundred miles of coast there were companies which sent open boats out to encircle the shoals of pilchards with seine nets. The pilchards were then taken ashore to pilchard 'palaces' where they were salted and packed into barrels for export. In 1859 the Great Western Railway built a bridge over the River Tamar and extended the railway net work into Cornwall. This allowed fresh fish to be sent to markets 'up country' and the fleets of 'driving' luggers were developed at the deep-water ports with a railhead. Most of these luggers were fitted with engines just before World War I.

103. The harbour at Polperro before World War I when about forty gaffers and luggers fished out of this gap in the cliffs. Polperro had repeated disasters caused by onshore southeasterly gales. In a really bad gale the spray will come right over the 90ft (27.43m) Peak, a rocky headland at the entrance, while other seas roll right up the cove destroying all the larger boats that could not be moved up into the streets. Several times the Polperro boats were destroyed and a new fleet had to be built.

The storm barrier of planks was lowered across the harbour mouth when a southeasterly gale rolled up into the cove. To operate the barrier needed eight men on the hand crane and two more on each end of the planks to get them in place for lowering. In 1978 an electric gate replaced the planks.

102. Left: The 88ft (26.82m) topsail schooner *Katie,* at Polruan on the Fowey River in the 1930s. Built by Stribley at Padstow in 1881 she became one of the fleet of sailing schooners owned by Stephens of Fowey. The *Katie* and the three-master *Mary Miller* went on carrying cargoes under sail until 1940. Later *Katie* was sold to owners in Denmark and sadly, in 1972, she sank in the Baltic when there was an attempt to bring her back to Cornwall for restoration.

Stephens' schooners depended on the Tregaskis yard at Par for maintenance. Benjamin Tregaskis had a tremendous knowledge about how to maintain the wooden vessels. He died aged ninety in 1949 and the yard closed in 1957. In North Devon the wooden motor-sail vessels operating from Appledore all relied on Harris' yard for maintenance.

104. On the right is the Tamar barge *PHE* discharging at East Looe in about 1937. These small barges came down the coast in the summer from Plymouth. Above the barge are the inshore fishing boats while the Looe fleet of motor luggers were at sea. At this time about two thousand Cornish men were fishermen. The coastal vessel *Bastin* was bringing Medway cement to Looe until about 1967.

105. The Tamar barge *Mayblossom* loading road stone at Steven Brothers' Teluggan Quarry on the Lynher River in about 1936. Captain Richard Hosking and his mate are returning aboard by boat. The Tamar barges carried cargoes along the coast between the Helford River and Weymouth, but they mostly worked near Plymouth. There was another fleet of barges, slightly finer lined, trading from Falmouth.

22. The 40ft (12.19m) Cornish lugger *Guide Me,* entering Looe in 1999. Built at Looe in 1911 as a pilchard driver (drifter) *Guide Me* is the home of Jon and Judy Brickhill who sail her without an engine. Because she is coming in under sail and oar anchors have been rigged on the bow and stern to control her progress if needed.

23. The 40ft (12.19m) Mevagissey lugger *Reliance,* built by Dick Pill at Gorran Haven in 1903, racing in the Looe Lugger Regatta, 2001. The dipping lug rig worked well for the drift net fishermen because when 'driving' (drifting) at night they could lower the masts to make the motion more comfortable.

24. The West Country trading ketch *Garlandstone* just after she was re-launched at Morwellham Quay following a major rebuild in 1998. The 76ft (23.17m) *Garlandstone* was originally built by James Goss in 1909, just down the River Tamar at Calstock. She became one of the motor ketches operated from Appledore in North Devon until she finished trading in 1958.

24a. The new wooden barque *Jeanie Johnston* at Fenit, County Kerry in 2002. The original *Jeanie Johnston* of Tralee carried many immigrants to North America without losing a passenger between 1847-58. This was during the devastating potato famine in the west of Ireland when death at sea was common place.

. The Portsmouth seine boat *Snowdrop* after her restoration by Dave Moore in 2001. The *Snowdrop* had been ilt by Feltham, at Portsmouth, for Dave Moore's grandfather in 1911 for £11. This boat, with its square-headed ping lugsail, was based in Langstone Harbour for seine netting.

. The 55ft (16.8) tripper boat *William Allchorn* hauled up on the beach at Easbourne in 2000. The 100-seater *lliam Allchorn* is the largest craft in Europe working off a beach. In the summer this craft and the 45ft 3.7m) *Southern Queen* make 45-minute trips down to Beachy Head. Allchorn Boats was started in 1860 and 1995 Brian Allchorn sold the business to Ron Keyte.

27. Jack Burnham beaching the *Lady Irene* on the South End beach, Deal in 2000. The *Lady Irene* was buil
in 1910 at Deal for taking trips off the beach in the summer. The Deal hovellers had been serving passing
sailing ships but steamers did not stop here so they changed to fishing and taking summer visitors on trips t
create incomes.

Tom Burnham started to buy up the Deal beach boats and keep them in their traditional part of the beach
Tom's twin sons Ben and Jack work these boats in inshore waters. This is a case of a family setting out t
preserve the local boats in their traditional setting.

Chapter Eight

UP CHANNEL AND ROUND THE NORTH FORELAND

Plymouth to the Isle of Sheppey

106. The Tamar barge *Lynher* at Morwellham Quay in 1998 after she had been rebuilt. The *Lynher,* built by Goss at Calstock in 1896, was one of three barges working from the Teluggan Quarry. She was fitted with an engine in 1926 and finally abandoned on the mud in 1952. Charlie Force dug the hulk out of the mud and took her to Morwellham Quay, where he totally rebuilt her over a period of six years. Another of these barges to be restored was the 57ft (17.37m) *Shamrock* built at Stonehouse, Plymouth in 1899 and now berthed at Cotehele Quay.

107. A recreation of the past. The West Country trading ketch *Garlandstone* on the slipway at the open-air museum at Morwellham Quay. Alan Williams and Tommi Neilsen & Co. rebuilt her here between 1991-98. She was just a bare hull when the rebuild started, and in order to find authentic pumps, Tommi Neilsen went down to Purton, on the River Severn near Sharpness. Here there are many hulks of wooden sailing vessels, and he found a set of pumps in one of these.

108. Above Right: A 28ft (8.53m) open three-masted Beer lugger in about 1910. The three-masted luggers were almost the first case of European collaboration because they were evolved for smuggling in the eighteenth century by the English and French builders of the eastern English Channel. The Brittany fishermen went on to perfect the three-master into a very fine sailing craft, but in British ports the mainmast was left ashore to create two-masted luggers. By the 1880s the only three-masted luggers in Britain were the open beach boats at Beer. The last one, *Beatrice Annie E80,* was trawling until 1917.

At Beer it is said that 'Beer made Brixham, Brixham made the North Sea'. The claim is that trawling was invented at Beer, then spread to Brixham. When the Brixham trawlermen and their families sailed up to Ramsgate and Lowestoft, trawling was introduced there. The Thames trawlermen left Barking Creek and moved to Great Yarmouth.

109. Right: Beer luggers racing on a Monday evening in 1987. The first boat at Beer was fitted with an engine in 1916 and the luggers faded out in the next decade. However, in about 1984 Alan Abbott, whose father and grandfather had been fishing under sail from Beer, thought of a way of reviving the local luggers for racing. Instead of lowering the dipping forelug on a tack, the sail is brailed up and hauled around forward of the mast. In this way a traditional boat type was made acceptable to modern racing people.

110. The boomie (ketch) barge *Lord Alcester* is being warped into West Bay, Bridport, a harbour which was sometimes closed by shingle piling up across the mouth. Three of her crew of five are resting, waiting for the flood tide to make a little more, so that the barge could float in. George Skinner of Woodbridge, whose father had owned the barge, said that she could load 295 tons of coal. The barge already has the cargo gaff aloft ready for the crew to start working the coal out of her in baskets.

Although she was a flat-bottomed barge, the *Lord Alcester* has the appearance of a trading ketch and she even appears to have a figurehead. This was because she was built by Harveys of Littlehampton who had built ocean-going sailing ships so that their barges were referred to as being 'schooners with the bottoms cut off'. Harveys launched the last of their thirty-four boomie barges, *Moultonian,* in 1919 after which the yard closed. The shipbuilder at West Bay, Elias Cox, was building ocean-going square-riggers until the yard closed in 1885.

111. Top Right: A four-oar lerret at Fortuneswell with the Isle of Portland in the background, 1981. The lerrets were originally spritsail rigged and went to France on smuggling trips, but by the end of the nineteenth century were used for inshore fishing.

This end of Chesil is called Dead Man's Bay because sailing ships that could not get past Portland Bill in a gale were driven ashore and wrecked here. Chesil Beach gets its name from Old English word of shingle. Chesil is a great bank of shingle that runs from the Isle of Portland for some eleven miles to the west. The sea has graded the shingle so that the large stones are at the Portland end and they get small as the beach runs to the west.

There was a belief that a lerret should not go to sea without, hanging in the bow, a lucky stone with a natural hole. Although there is no longer fishing at Abbotsbury they still hold the Garland Day on the Old May Day (May 13) which was the start of the mackerel season. The boats once put to sea and threw a garland of flowers into the sea, a survival of sea god worship.

12. A paddle steamer taking on passengers in Lulworth Cove in about 1930. Some South Coast steamers ran summer trips across to the Channel Islands.

113. The Floating Bridge ferry linking Cowes with East Cowes in about 1910. Yachting began on the Thames in the eighteenth century with the Cumberland Fleet, but in the nineteenth century the increasing commercialization drove yachts away. Yachtsmen boarded the railway trains and travelled down to the South Coast to make Cowes the new yachting centre.

114. Above Right: A Back of the Wight mackerel boat at Blackgang Chine in 1910. Most of the men are Wheelers and their relations. The Wheelers once caught two shoals with their seine net and landed 18,000 mackerel. However the fishery was exhausted by the 1950s and the boats were left to rot on the clifftop.

Although it is a very inhospitable place to work a boat from, there were many small beach landings on the English Channel side of the Isle of Wight. There was a tiny beach landing at Castle Haven very near to St Catherine's Point. The lane down to this had to be wide enough for two wagons to pass when ships brought coal on to the open beach. There was a simple breakwater, made of posts with stones piled between them. This is how the first medieval harbours started. There was a long and successful agreement between the landowner and the fishermen that if they kept the breakwater up and maintained the lane they could use the beach for nothing.

The beach landings to the east of St Catherine's are slightly more sheltered and there is a mild climate on Undercliff, running from Niton to Ventnor, which attracted visitors. This led to the resorts along this coast having pleasure craft operating off the beaches in the summer.

115. Right: An Old Gaffers' Race at St Aubin, Jersey. Left to right: *Providence, Morvorer,* Essex smack *Shamrock* and *Cilara.* The Old Gaffers' Association was formed in 1963 at a time when the gaff rig was going out of fashion and through its races managed to promote this rig again.

17. The Brighton pleasure boat *Skylark* returning to the beach loaded with trippers. In the early nineteenth century there were four hundred fishermen working off Brighton beach. Fresh mackerel landed here could be London within eight hours by using post-chase horses. The early nineteenth century Brighton boats were known as 'hog boats' or 'hoggies' and were 28ft (8.53m) long, but had an incredible 16ft (4.87m) beam so that they rode through the surf like fat ducks. In the 1880s the hoggies were replaced with luggers similar to the Hastings boats and later fishermen started buying Cornish luggers and working them from Shoreham. Although fishing faded out, the Fishing Museum was started and in 1980 the annual 'Blessing the Nets' was started. This later became the Mackerel Fayre, which is a local event and fishing boats sometimes come and anchor off the beach.

16. Left: Brighton fishermen repairing a trawl net on a 'hoggie' lugger in 1871. In the nineteenth century Worthing, Brighton, Eastbourne and Hastings all had luggers working off the open beaches. These had to be hauled up the beach by hand capstans at the end of each trip, but in spite of the difficulties, Brighton had its own fish market. When engines were adopted, most of the West Sussex fishermen moved to Shoreham Harbour. By 1930 the Brighton luggers *Belinda* and *Elizabeth II* were up for sale. Since there were no buyers the owner, Johnson, gave them to his skipper George Andrews and they were burnt on the beach in 1940 so that they did not get in the line of fire if there was an invasion.

The last lugger working under sail at Brighton was the 27ft (7.63m) *Victory*. Her elderly skipper, Alfred Cobbett, refused to have an engine, although often when the wind dropped the *Victory* had to be rowed home with 17ft (5.18m) sweeps. Cobbett never wore gloves, but kept his hands hard by rubbing them with rock salt. He used to go down to Rye Bay for plaice and sole. He had a glass-bottomed bucket and used it to look down into the water as he knew which channels the fish swam through during the different seasons of the year. Like most of the Brighton fishermen, Cobbett lived in Kemp Town and used to buy meals from the Miss Blanchs, who had a café in Edward Street. These meals were reheated over the cuddy stove and then the cooking bowls returned.

These were not the last deck boats at Brighton. In 1939 the *May Queen* was built by E. Phillips at Rye and the *Mizpah* was built at Newhaven for Brighton owners. But fishing died out and the last large fishing craft on the beach was Alan Haze's 24ft (7.31m) *Peace & Plenty,* until 1976, and the last part-time fishermen gave up in 1995.

118. Net mending on the elliptical-sterned *Seeker* at Eastbourne in 1981. The two Sussex builders, R. Lowe & Son at Newhaven, which was started in 1947, and H.L. Phillips and Son of Rye used to build elliptical the older lute-stern according to the owner's requirements. The last boat Lower built was the Eastbourne *Nguyen Van Tromi,* named after a Vietnamese leader, in 1977. In 1984 Lower and Street built the 27ft (8.23m *Searcher* for Brian Skinner to work off Eastbourne beach. She was powered by a 47hp Gardner diesel and wa intended to fish around the wrecks up to twelve miles offshore. The same year Lower and Street built wooden 17ft (5.18m) lute-sterned boat for Norman Bashford to fish from Worthing beach.

Phillips was founded in 1904 and built hundreds of wooden beach 'punts', in a shed on the Rock Channe Rye until about 1985. Derek Phillips then built a 26ft (7.92m) class of GRP boats with elliptical sterns. 2000, Phillips built their first boat for ten years, the 26ft *Coptic,* a traditional open boat with a mizzen, fe William Richardson to fish off the Sussex beaches.

119. The Hastings lugger *Surprise,* built at Hastings in 1904, beaching in bad weather. All boats landing on open beaches run the risk of being swamped, even the decked craft. Because the Sussex boats always beached bow first and launched off stern first they developed the extended 'lute' stern so that the sea rolling on to the beach got under the stern and lifted the craft.

In the early nineteenth century Hastings had been a major fishing station with a fleet of 55ft (16.76m) three-masted luggers that followed the herring shoals up to Great Yarmouth. These luggers were fast, fine-lined craft that were only pulled ashore at the end of the fishing season. Then they were hauled up beside the tall net shops so that the gear could be taken straight into them across a plank from the lugger's decks.

The three-masted Hastings luggers were replaced in about 1870 by the small decked two-masted luggers, like the *Surprise*. These just fished close to Hastings and had very beamy hulls to give more buoyancy when beaching in bad weather. Eastbourne also had a fleet of three-masted luggers, which went as far as southern Ireland, but here the Victorian hotel owners drove the fishermen off the beach. They literally hired a steam traction engine to go along and smash up the boats, but at Hastings the fishermen were able to prove they owned the Stade beach and the local council has not been able to evict them.

121. The Hastings fishing boats ashore in bad weather during 1966 with the Fish Market and Net Shops in the foreground. The decked Big Boats were all trawlers, but when the Hastings men switched to trammel netting in Rye Bay the open 20ft (6.09m) punts became more economical. In 1982 there were forty-two boats working off Hastings beach and this was the largest number at any beach landing in the British Isles.

The Net Shops provided a way of saving space when there was less beach. The three-masted luggers, between herring and mackerel voyages, were hauled ashore and the gear carried across a plank at deck level to the Net Shops.

120. Left: The elliptical-sterned *Mayflower* and *Breadwinner* on Hastings beach in about 1947. Although they had engines, these beach boats are still fully rigged in much the same way as the Victorian sailing luggers. The Hastings boats did not give up sails until reliable diesel engines became available in the 1950s.

The first Sussex elliptical-sterned craft was the *Clupidae* in 1892 and this hull shape was an attempt to copy the counter sterns on the racing yachts of the period. The last clinker sailing lugger built at Hastings was the 28ft *Mayflower* in 1913. After this Hastings boats were fitted with engines and the first power craft, the 28ft *Edward & Mary* built in 1919, had a 13hp petrol/paraffin Kelvin engine and lug sails.

By 1964 all the former sailing and auxiliary sailing boats had been replaced by decked Big Boats. Only one further Big Boat was built, the 31ft (9.45m) *Our Pam and Peter* by H.L. Phillips at Rye for Denis Barton in 1982, while most of the new boats were 20-23ft (6.09-7.01m) open punts. Hastings has the largest fleet of inshore fishing boats and some new steel beach boats have joined the fleet, notably the Adams' *Hayley William Henry* and in 1999 the *Bethan Louise.*

122. Kettle fishing on the sands of Rye Bay in about 1937. This was the form of fish trap that gave rise to the saying 'A pretty kettle of fish'. The traps were used in various forms in the bays and estuaries all around the coast of the British Isles. The Rye Bay kettle nets or 'keddles' were used in June and the fish retailed at Winchelsea. By 2001 only 'Jimper' Sutton was still working the keddle nets and he also had his own back yard smokehouse for curing fish.

124. The tripper boat *Clarendon,* packed with trippers, being launched off North End beach, Deal in about 1911. This beach, now almost eroded away, was home to most of the Deal luggers. Groups of beachmen operated a 'set' of boats for different purposes. The 40ft luggers, known as 'forepeakers' because of their tiny cabin forward, went down the English Channel putting pilots on incoming ships. The open 'cat boats' took anchors out to ships at anchor, while smaller open 'galley punts', sailing boats that could be rowed, and 'galleys', rowing boats that could be sailed, were used for going alongside ships. These small boats had a short mast amidships, so that the mast did not catch the ship's spars as they went alongside, and they set a single very square lugsail.

123. Left: Deal boatmen leaning on a capstan in 1886 in their fine weather gear. Keeping warm was a major part of beachmen's lives. In wet weather the men wore oilskin trousers that reached up to their armpits and long oilskin coats that went down to their knees. No buttons were used, only rope lashing. Underneath these, heavy pilot cloth jackets and trousers were worn and leather wellington boots that were warmer that the modern rubber boots. Long woollen scarves, often three metres long, also protected their necks. In bad weather sou'westers, the great Victorian contribution to western civilization, were worn, but in fine weather the Deal men proudly donned their sealskin caps.

The hand capstans at Deal were powerful enough to pull a 40ft (12.19m) lugger up the beach. In the age of sail, The Downs, a sheltered piece of the Straits of Dover just to the north of Deal, was an important anchorage for both merchant and Royal Navy vessels. The beachmen took supplies out to the large fleets that gathered in the Downs waiting for fine weather to go out into the North Sea or the English Channel. In bad weather the Deal hovellers went out and salvaged vessels that were in trouble.

127. Sailing barges being loaded with gunpowder at the head of Oare Creek. The gunpowder works were moved down from the Thames in Elizabethan times to the lonely marshes of north Kent.

125. Above Left: The spritsail barge *Onward* on the Horsebridge at Whitstable. The Horsebridge was a hard area on the foreshore, created in about 1500, where ships could lie to discharge between tides. After the small harbour was built barges continued to use the Horsebridge, until 1939, in fine weather because they did not have to pay harbour dues. A northerly gale could drive the sea right into Whitstable's harbour so that the oyster smacks were often taken out and anchored in the open Thames Estuary to avoid damage. The smacks used to lie off Whitstable in a gale and water rolled right across their decks.

126. Left: A barge sailing out of Whitstable with colliers lying on the harbour entrance pier in about 1902. Whitstable had a fleet of around thirty rather elderly square-rigged colliers bringing coal from the north of England. Their crews complained that 'the Whitstable men pumped up chalk ballast when bound north and coal dust when bound south'. The Whitstable colliers just lasted into the 1920s because they had a small financial advantage, in that they could sail right up to the pier and warp themselves into the harbour. The schooners and brigantines owned in Sussex ports usually had to hire a tug. The Bull Line of Shoreham sold all their sailing colliers in 1907 while Littlehampton's last collier, the brigantine *Ebenezer*, was sold in 1915.

Chapter Nine

WORK ON THE SHORE

128. Boys hand trawling for shrimp at Hastings, 1903. There were enough shrimp near the beach for this to be done commerically around many beaches until after World War II.

129. Discharging and weighing potatoes by hand at Mill Dam Quay, South Shields, 1910.

130. Women gutting herring at Lowestoft about 1911. The men packed and moved the barrels.

131. Woman raking the foreshore for cockles in the River Exe, Devon. Women here and on the North Norfolk coast did this work bare-footed.

Also from Creekside Publishing by Robert Simper.

English Estuaries Series

DEBEN RIVER
RIVER ORWELL AND RIVER STOUR
RIVERS ALDE, ORE AND BLYTH
NORFOLK RIVERS AND HARBOURS
ESSEX RIVERS AND CREEKS
THAMES TIDEWAY
RIVER MEDWAY AND THE SWALE
RIVERS TO THE FENS

The Sea and the Land books
IN SEARCH OF SAIL
FAMILY FIELDS
VOYAGE AROUND EAST ANGLIA
WOODBRIDGE & BEYOND